EOG
Reading and Writing

Steck-Vaughn Edition

Copyright © by Harcourt Brace & Company

Test Best® is a registered trademark of Steck-Vaughn Company.

ISBN 0-7398-7359-8

1 2 3 4 5 6 7 8 9 10   10 09 08 07 06 05 04 03 02

STECK-VAUGHN
A Harcourt Company

www.steck-vaughn.com

Name _____

Directions: Read the selection and answer the questions.

Let me tell you about my horse, Susie-Q. She's part Arab, part quarter horse, and all spirit. She's short, like me, but she can outrun all the other horses where I ride. She never needs much urging; in fact, my arms are often sore after a trail ride because I've been holding her back from a hard gallop.

Susie-Q is a beautiful chestnut color. She has a white blaze on her face and one matching white "stocking" on her right hind leg. Because of her breeding, every inch of her is well muscled. What I like best about Susie-Q, though, is how she looks when the sun shines on her after she's been washed and groomed. The golden red color of her coat looks like freshly polished copper, and her white markings seem to glow in contrast. Somehow, she seems to know how good-looking she is, because she'll prance and arch her neck proudly. Of course, if I'm not careful, she'll also try to roll in the dirt. Horses love to do that after a bath if they can get away with it!

In the riding ring, Susie-Q is well behaved—most of the time! I remember one local horse show in the fall. We had to race to the other end of the ring, jump off our horses, and bob for apples in big metal tubs full of water. The ring was quite small from end to end.

When the starter said "Go!" Susie plunged right into a full gallop, practically throwing me out of the saddle. She barreled down toward the fence at the other end of the ring. All I could ask myself was, "Is this

horse going to stop, or am I going headfirst into that fence?" Somehow, I got her to dig in her heels and stop at the last possible second. At that point, she had finished her part of the race, and we were in first place.

Now it was my turn to jump off and bob for an apple. I had to keep my hands behind my back and open my mouth real wide to snatch one. By the time I got it, we were in last place in the race! Maybe the horse should've done the running and the bobbing! (I did give her the apple, though.)

Susie's smart, too. She makes herself just about impossible to catch in the paddock, a pen for animals. It helps if you know the secret call, which in her language means "oats—come and get 'em!" I've cut way back on her ration of oats, because she has so much natural energy. Too many oats or other grains can make a horse "hot" and difficult to handle.

Susie has also learned every horse's favorite trick: "If I hold my breath, maybe they won't put the saddle on me after all."

A horse will bloat its stomach, making it difficult to tighten the saddle strap that goes around its belly. What a surprise for the unwary rider when the saddle slides off during a trail ride! To outsmart Susie-Q when she's trying to outsmart me, I have to press my knee firmly into her left side as I'm tightening the saddle strap that goes under her. It's quite a juggling act for me, but a ride on Susie-Q is worth it.

Constructing Meaning

1. Describe Susie-Q in detail, using information from the selection.

_____

_____

_____

_____

_____

_____

_____

2. List three things that the narrator did with Susie-Q in the local horse show.

   a. _____

   b. _____

   c. _____

3. Is the narrator proud of Susie-Q? Use information from the selection to support your answer.

_____

_____

_____

_____

_____

© Harcourt

Extending Meaning

1. **Fill in the Venn diagram with a word to describe Susie-Q, a word to describe the narrator, and a word to describe them both. Use a word only once. Choose from:**

spirited

clever

patient

fast

lively

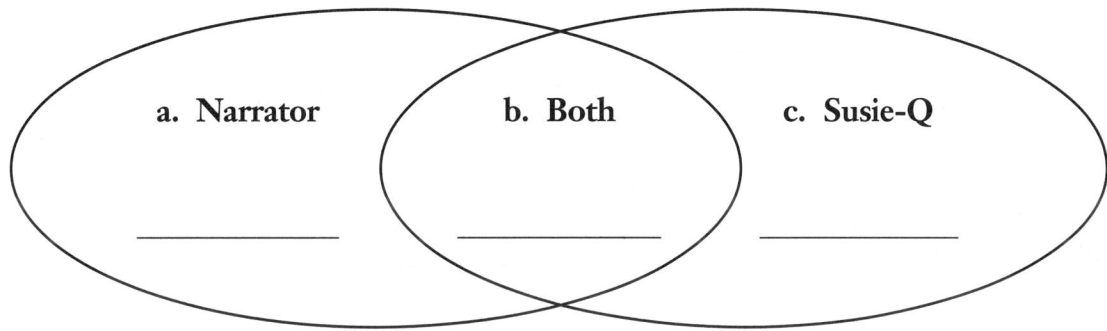

a. **Narrator**   b. **Both**   c. **Susie-Q**

_____   _____   _____

2. **Does the narrator think Susie-Q is worth all of the hard work? Use information from the selection to support your answer.**

_____

_____

_____

_____

_____

_____

_____

_____

_____

Practice Test

Directions: Choose the best answer and fill in the circle of your choice.

1. What is the meaning of the word *paddock* in the sixth paragraph in the selection?

   (A) stable

   (B) fencing

   (C) a pen for animals

   (D) container for oats

2. To saddle a horse that is holding its breath, _____.

   (A) press the saddle against its back

   (B) wait for it to take a breath

   (C) tighten the saddle with a special tool

   (D) press one knee firmly into the horse's left side

3. Which statement expresses the main idea of the selection?

   (A) Bobbing for apples is fun for a horse.

   (B) Some horses are stronger than others.

   (C) Susie-Q is fast, smart, and spirited.

   (D) People like to ride and care for horses.

4. When Susie-Q reached the end of the riding ring, _____.

   (A) the narrator fed her oats

   (B) she stopped just before the fence

   (C) she ate the apple

   (D) she jumped the fence

5. It is important to know your horse's personality because _____.

   (A) they are like people

   (B) a horse is not very smart

   (C) some horses like to race, and some do not

   (D) it helps you to anticipate how your horse will react in new situations

6. Eating too many oats can cause a horse to _____.

   (A) lose weight

   (B) have too much energy

   (C) stop eating apples

   (D) become sleepy

GO ON

7. What does the narrator mean by saying Susie-Q is "all spirit" in the first paragraph?

_____

_____

_____

8. What does the narrator like best about Susie-Q?

_____

_____

_____

9. Fill in the cause-and-effect chart using information from the selection.

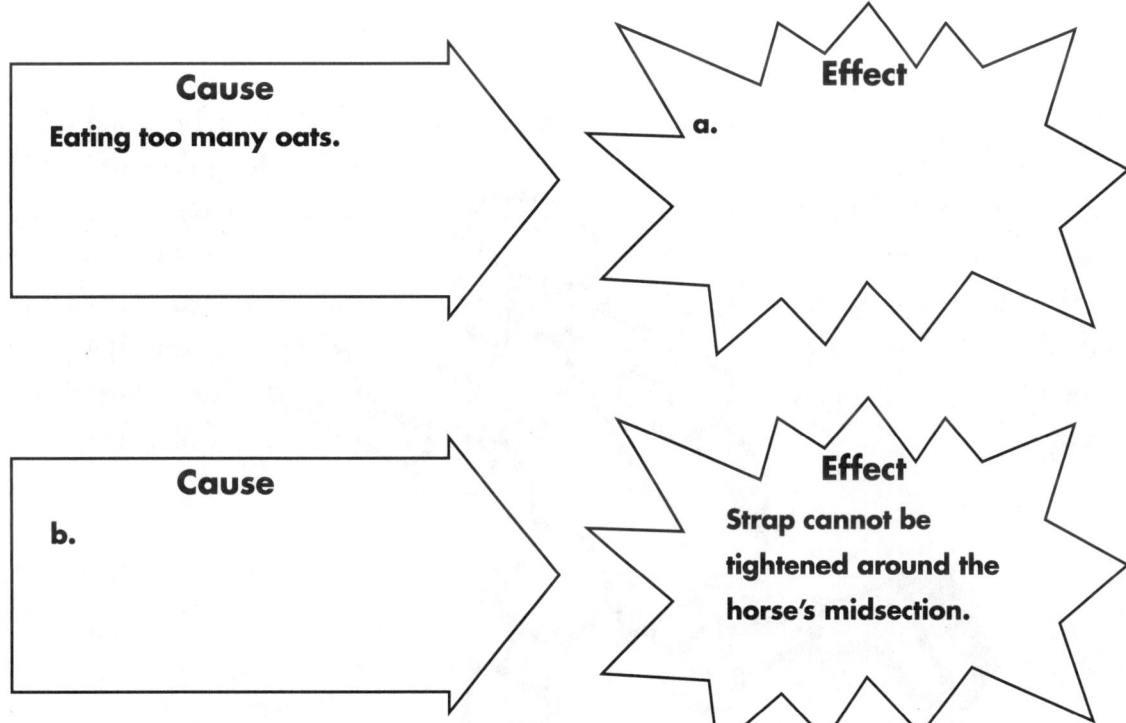

Cause
Eating too many oats.

Effect
a.

Cause
b.

Effect
Strap cannot be tightened around the horse's midsection.

STOP

Name _____

Directions: Read the selection and answer the questions.

Do you enjoy roller-skating but want something new and more challenging? Then in-line skating, or blading, is probably for you. This sport combines the best of ice-skating and roller-skating to create a sport that is more difficult than roller-skating but more accessible than ice-skating.

In-line skates have three to five wheels in a row down the middle of a boot sole. The boot is made of molded plastic or polyurethane. The more wheels on the skates, the faster you can go. These skates are more maneuverable than traditional roller skates that have two sets of parallel wheels.

In-line skating was introduced in 1980 as an off-season training tool for hockey players. In 1986, a Minnesota company redesigned the in-line skates used in training, and soon they became popular with other groups.

The United States Ski Team uses them for cross-training. Today the skates are attracting runners, cyclists, ice-skaters, injured athletes, tennis and basketball players, as well as many sports amateurs.

Blading, however, requires some caution. One of the main causes of falls is an inability to stop. Unlike traditional roller skates, in-line skates have a round rubberlike stopper at the heel of one skate. You have to flex your foot in order to stop. Needless to say, knee pads, elbow pads, helmets, and wrist guards are recommended.

Unfortunately, as with any new fad, the equipment is expensive. The cost of in-line skates ranges from $70 to $350 a pair. Standard roller skates cost about $9 to $24 a pair. Many places rent the new in-line skates for a reasonable rate, and as the fad diminishes, so should the price. After all, roller skates have been around since the eighteenth century. They enjoyed their greatest popularity between 1909 and 1912 and again in 1929. The price of roller skates has dropped since they were at the height of their popularity. We can assume the price of in-line skates will do the same.

Constructing Meaning

1. Use the Venn diagram to compare and contrast in-line skates and traditional roller skates.

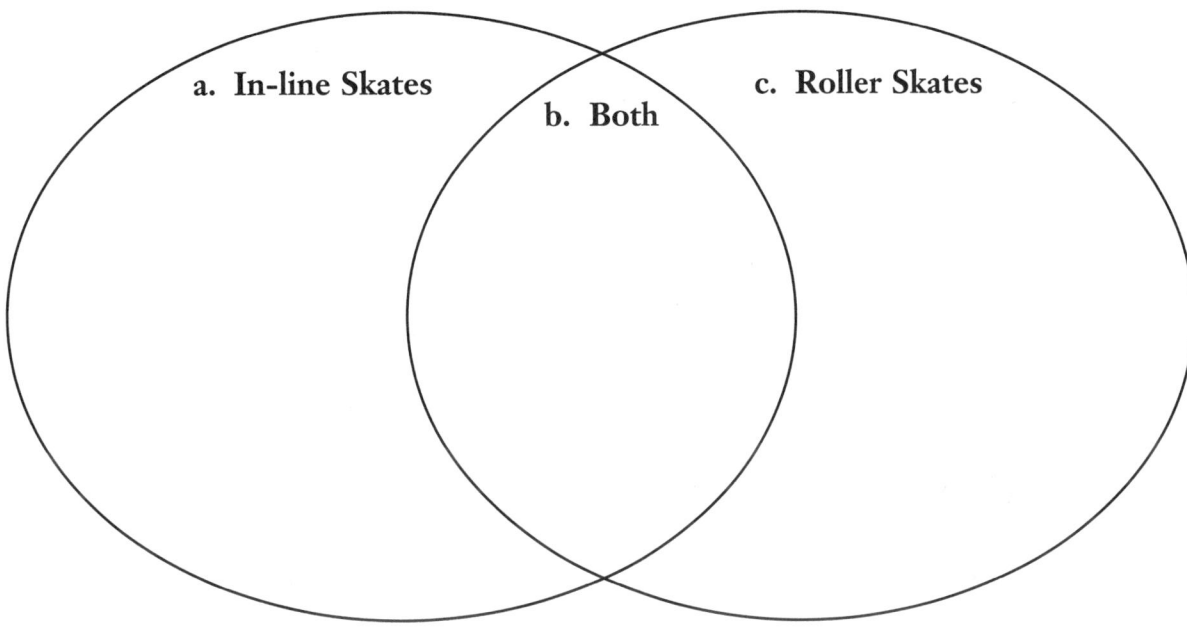

2. Would you recommend roller-skating or blading to a friend? Explain your answer.

_____

_____

_____

_____

_____

_____

_____

_____

_____

_____

Name _____

Extending Meaning

1. Does the author think that the price of in-line skates will increase or decrease? Support your answer with information from the selection.

_____

_____

_____

_____

_____

_____

2. In which of the following sources could you find information on the history of the sport of blading: *Blading, Then and Now* or *Skating Magazine*? Support your answer.

_____

_____

_____

_____

_____

_____

Practice Test

Directions: Choose the best answer and fill in the circle of your choice.

1. When did roller skates first become popular?

   (A) in 1986

   (B) between 1909 and 1912

   (C) during the 1970s

   (D) in 1929

2. Which of these is an opinion stated in the selection?

   (A) Roller-skating is less challenging than in-line skating.

   (B) In-line skates have three to five wheels.

   (C) The more wheels on the skates, the faster they can go.

   (D) In-line skating was introduced in 1980.

3. Which of these is the best summary of the selection?

   (A) Roller-skating was most popular between 1909 and 1912.

   (B) The price of roller skates has dropped since they were at their height of popularity.

   (C) As with any fad, the equipment is expensive.

   (D) In-line skating is a popular new sport for professional and amateur athletes.

4. What is the meaning of the word *blading* in the selection?

   (A) ice-skating

   (B) in-line skating

   (C) roller-skating

   (D) skateboarding

5. Besides the wheels, what is the difference between the two skates pictured in Figures 1 and 2?

   (A) The roller skate has a toe stop; the in-line skate has a heel stop.

   (B) The laces are tied differently on the skates.

   (C) The width of the roller skate is greater.

   (D) The length of the in-line skate is greater.

Fig. 1   Fig. 2

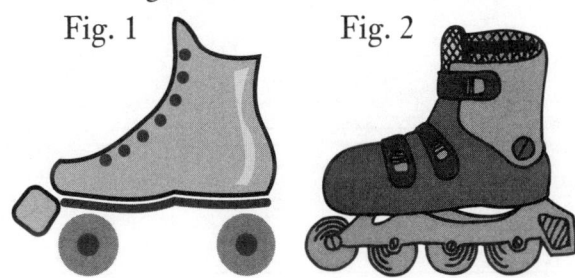

6. The cost of athletic equipment seems to be related to a sport's _____.

   (A) name

   (B) difficulty

   (C) popularity

   (D) history

GO ON

7. According to the selection, why would someone who enjoys roller-skating want to try blading?

_____

_____

_____

_____

_____

_____

_____

_____

8. In the context of the selection, what does the word *fad* mean in the last paragraph?

_____

_____

_____

_____

_____

_____

_____

_____

© Harcourt

STOP

Name _____

Directions: Follow along while this selection is read aloud to you.

Tricks and Triumphs of Archaeology

Through archaeology people learn about civilizations that existed many hundreds of thousands of years ago. Archaeologists recover objects and study dwellings that belonged to ancient peoples. They use historical sources and scientific techniques to form a picture of when and how artifacts from long ago were used.

How do archaeologists know where to begin hunting for "buried treasure"? They read our oldest written records, such as ancient poetry, the Bible, or other historical works. For example, a man named Heinrich Schliemann (1822–1890) was fascinated by Homer's account of the Trojan War. Homer was a Greek poet who lived more than 3,000 years ago. Clues in the poem led Schliemann to the ancient state of Troy, in Turkey. He found a Trojan fortress, proving that Homer's *Iliad* was based on a real war.

Before starting an excavation, archaeologists study an area and form a plan. They then bore or dig into the earth and decide how big an excavation site should be. Sometimes, digging machines safely remove the topsoil. But most of the work is done by hand with shovels and trowels.

As each object comes to light, archaeologists make a precise record of where it was found. They may make scale drawings and contour maps of the site. These sketches show how far down in the earth each object was buried. The artifacts are then cleaned and studied.

Underwater archaeology is a growing field. Using scuba-diving equipment, divers explore lake bottoms and ocean floors. One team found a prehistoric site near Israel. A number of sailing vessels, including the ships of Mediterranean merchants, have been recovered in other places.

Archaeologists try to figure out the age of objects. This can be done by cross-dating, or comparing artifacts from one culture with those of another. Another technique is radiocarbon dating, in which scientists measure the radioactive carbon-14 content of material that was once alive. This method can show the age of artifacts that might have been made as long as 50,000 years ago. As new dating techniques are found, archaeologists will be able to tell us still more about the past.

Writing

Pre-writing

You will use the ideas from the selection to help you complete two writing activities. For the first activity, you will write an informational report on archaeology. For the second activity, you will write a news report about an archaeological discovery.

Directions: The flowchart below will help you organize ideas from the passage in order to write your informational report. Fill in the boxes with information about the process of excavating explained in the passage "Tricks and Triumphs of Archaeology."

STEP 1: Before the Excavation

_____

_____

_____

STEP 2: During the Excavation

_____

_____

_____

STEP 3: After the Excavation

_____

_____

_____

Name _____

Pre-writing

Directions: Use the graphic organizer to identify the answers to key questions about the archaeological discovery for your news report.

Event: My archaeological discovery

Who discovered it?

What was discovered?

Where was it discovered?

When was it discovered?

How was it discovered?

Why is this discovery important?

© Harcourt

Informational Essay

Directions: For this exercise, you will write an informational essay in which you describe archaeology. You may use the ideas that you wrote on previous pages. Be sure to use descriptive words. Include details and information from the passage "Tricks and Triumphs of Archaeology." Be sure to use words that make your meaning clear. Be sure that your informational essay is well organized and complete.

Look at the box below. The checklist shows what your writing must have to receive your best score.

Checklist

I will earn my best score if:

⇨ My informational essay describes archaeology.

⇨ My informational essay includes information from the passage.

⇨ My informational essay is well organized and complete.

⇨ I use words that make my meaning clear in my informational essay, and I do not use the same words over and over.

⇨ I spell words correctly.

⇨ I use correct punctuation and capitalization.

© Harcourt

News Report

Directions: For this exercise, you will write a news report about an archaeological discovery. You may use the ideas that you wrote on previous pages. Explain why the discovery is interesting or important. Be sure your report answers the key questions: *Who, What, Where, When, Why*, and *How*. Answer the questions in the order of their importance.

Look at the box below. The checklist shows what your writing must have to receive your best score.

Checklist

I will earn my best score if:

⇨ My news report identifies a discovery.

⇨ My news report explains why the discovery is interesting or important.

⇨ My news report answers the key questions *Who, What, Where, When, Why*, and *How*.

⇨ My report provides information in the order of its importance.

⇨ My report is well organized and complete.

⇨ I use a variety of words and sentence patterns, and I do not use the same words over and over.

⇨ I use correct spelling, punctuation, and capitalization.

Name _____

Directions: Read the selection and answer the questions.

Who would have thought that a little creature like a baby *Peromyscus maniculatus*, a deer mouse, could have caused such a stir in our household? My brother and I were watching an after-school TV show. Dad was still at work. Mom was trying to relax after a hectic commute from the city. It was then that she informed us that, out of the corner of her eye, she had seen something moving.

"Carol, I think it's a mouse," she said with a strange tone in her voice.

"Ridiculous!" I replied. "How could we have mice? We have two cats! Mom, are you sure you're not seeing things?" Noticing Mom's expression, I decided to humor her. I got up to investigate.

Sure enough, there it was, and there it went, scurrying around the room. My brother and I followed the tiny creature. It tried to hide behind one of the sneakers Mom had left by the desk in the corner of the family room. Then it was off and running again, this time to the opposite side of the room, behind the sofa. We chased the poor thing around the room several times. It must have been exhausted. I know we were.

"Travis, go get a box," I ordered. I was trying to take charge of the situation. "Let's see if we can catch it." Armed with leather gloves and a box, we tried again.

We tried to approach the mouse quietly. It heard us anyway and dashed under the chair next to where Mom was sitting. I was not prepared for what happened next. Mom gulped and then jumped onto the armchair. She just stood there—on the chair—looking down at my brother and me

as we looked up at her in total amazement. Our mom, who isn't afraid of anything, offered a rather lame excuse.

"It's not that I'm scared, mind you," she said. "I just don't want to step on it." Travis and I tried not to giggle, but we couldn't help it.

We set out after our little visitor again. This was getting silly. Finally, it ran into the bathroom and Travis closed the door. There was no way it could possibly escape. As I started to move toward the corner, it ran toward me and into the box!

Poor mouse. It just huddled in the box, looking up at the three of us. Mom had come down from the chair by then. The mouse just shook. I talked to it quietly, trying to reassure it that we meant it no harm. Even Mom took pity. She opened the box and put in some of the sunflower seeds she keeps for the birds she feeds. That's probably what it had been after in the first place. Every bird and squirrel in the neighborhood visits our yard for Mom's seeds. This creature probably figured that since it was getting cold, it could come inside to eat. Anyway, we let it calm down. I really wanted to keep it, but Mom insisted that I take it to the woods and let it go. Reluctantly, I did so.

Where were our two cats during this commotion? Well, they were asleep on my bed, probably dreaming about catching a mouse!

© Harcourt

Name _____

Constructing Meaning

1. Write a brief summary of the selection. Remember that when you summarize, you tell a shortened version of the original text in your own words. You should give only the most important information from the selection.

_____

_____

_____

_____

_____

_____

_____

_____

_____

_____

2. What is the narrator's attitude toward the mouse in this selection? Explain your answer.

_____

_____

_____

_____

_____

_____

_____

_____

_____

_____

© Harcourt

Extending Meaning

1. **Reread the selection. Then complete the story map.**

a. **Characters:**

b. **Setting:**

c. **Events:**

d. **Conclusion:**

2. **Did you enjoy reading this selection? Why or why not?**

_____

_____

_____

_____

_____

_____

© Harcourt

Practice Test

Directions: Choose the best answer and fill in the circle of your choice.

1. What is the meaning of the words *Peromyscus maniculatus* as they are used in the first sentence of the selection?

   (A) cats

   (B) deer mouse

   (C) mole

   (D) chipmunk

2. Where does this selection take place?

   (A) a campsite near the woods

   (B) an apartment in the city

   (C) a home in the suburbs

   (D) the grandparent's home

3. At what time of the day does the selection take place?

   (A) morning

   (B) noontime

   (C) midnight

   (D) evening

4. You can tell that the author of this selection thinks _____.

   (A) it's silly to let a mouse upset a household

   (B) a deer mouse is a dangerous animal

   (C) the cats should have slept all afternoon

   (D) giving a deer mouse some food is not a good idea

5. Which of these best describes the children in this selection?

   (A) extremely cautious

   (B) totally fearless

   (C) quite curious

   (D) indifferent

6. The main idea of this story is to show that a mouse _____.

   (A) is a harmful rodent

   (B) can create a humorous reaction with its presence

   (C) can easily get into your home

   (D) can easily escape detection by cats

GO ON

7. Fill in the Venn diagram with a word to describe the narrator, a word to describe the mouse, and a word to describe them both. Use each word only once. Choose from:

frightened

brave

exhausted

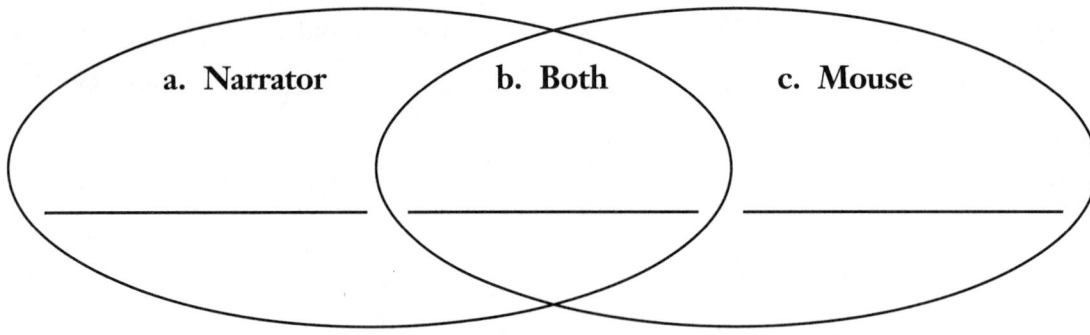

a. **Narrator**   b. **Both**   c. **Mouse**

8. Retell this story in detail.

_____

_____

_____

_____

_____

_____

_____

_____

_____

_____

_____

_____

_____

STOP

Directions: Read the selection and answer the questions.

Collecting has become an American craze. People from coast to coast are involved in some form of it. Some are collecting more traditional items, such as stamps, baseball cards, and coins. Others are collecting key chains, posters, patches, postcards, or autographs. The reasons for collecting are as varied as the forms. Some people do it for fun; others do it for money.

I've become a collector, too. My passion is comic books. Undoubtedly, comics are the most interesting and entertaining of all collectibles. Comic magazines combine art with storytelling. There are comics to fit anyone's reading taste: fantasy, realism, super hero/heroine, science fiction, or adventure stories. The stories make great reading because they are always action-packed. Also, a comic book never takes very long to read.

If comic-book collecting sounds interesting, maybe it's the hobby for you. I like to buy a magazine, read it, save it for a few months, and then trade it. Since today's titles cost between $0.75 and $1.75, I don't have to spend a lot of money. I try to buy at least ten new comics a month, but sometimes I have trouble choosing! Bookstores and comic-book shows are good places to find new titles. Mostly, I trade my comics with friends or people I meet at shows. Because I am bilingual, I sometimes trade my American comics with my Mexican pen pal.

If you decide to become a serious comic-book collector, you have to invest some time before you invest money. Begin by reading a variety of old and new comics. Comics were started in the 1930s, so don't forget to look at the earliest ones. Decide which stories, characters, and titles are your favorites. Then read guidebooks and newsletters and talk to other collectors about the hobby. Once you've done your homework, the fun of collecting begins.

Look for new titles at comic-book shows. Go to yard sales and rare-book shops if you are in search of older comics. Read newspaper ads, too; collectors often want to sell or trade. Once you have located a comic you want, look at it carefully. Comics are rated mint, fine, and good condition. The better the condition, the more valuable the comic. Be aware that the fewer issues there are of a title, the more costly that title is. Older comics sometimes bring a higher price than newer ones.

Once you are ready to sell or trade a comic, first check its value. This will ensure that you make a profit or receive a fair trade. Remember, too, that whether collecting for fun or for profit, a good comic-book collector always enjoys the experience!

Name _____

Constructing Meaning

1. Do you think the author of this selection enjoys collecting comic books? Explain your answer.

_____

_____

_____

_____

_____

_____

_____

_____

2. Use the Venn diagram to compare and contrast collecting comic books for fun and collecting comic books for profit.

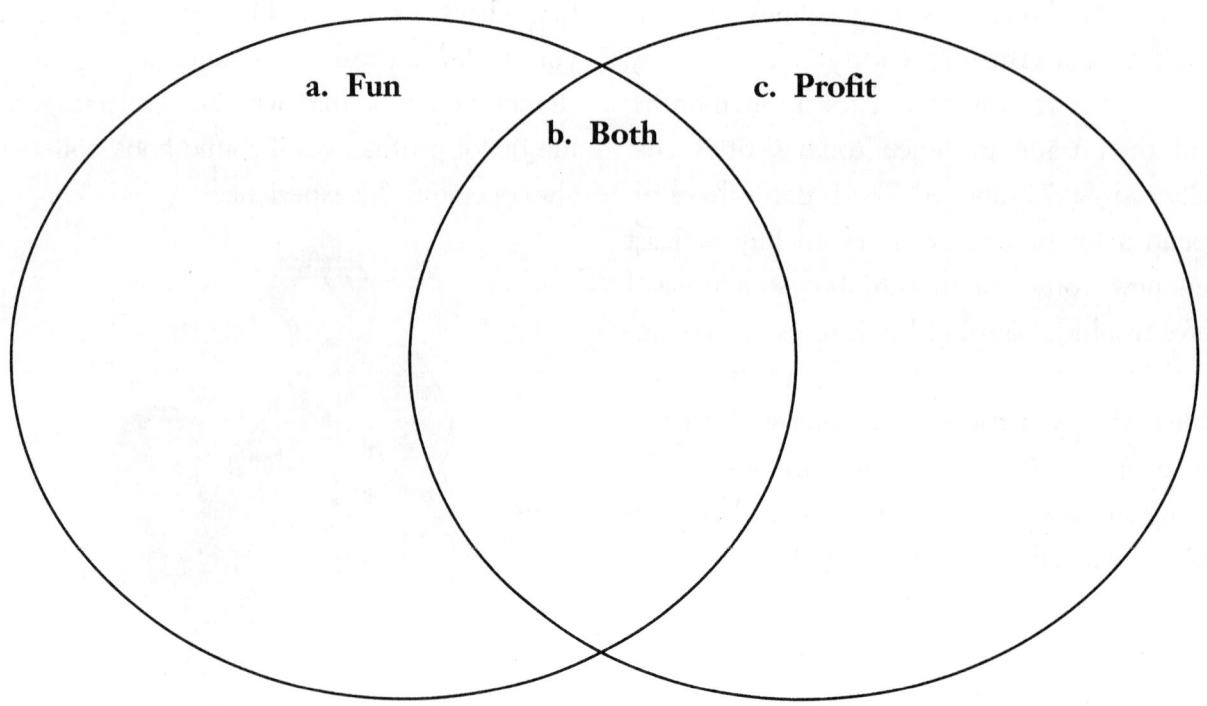

a. Fun

b. Both

c. Profit

© Harcourt

Extending Meaning

1. In which of the following sources could a person find other people who are interested in buying and selling comic books: a newspaper or *The History of Comic Books*? Explain your answer.

_____

_____

_____

_____

_____

_____

_____

2. Does the author convince you that comic-book collecting is fun? Why or why not?

_____

_____

_____

_____

_____

_____

_____

Reading

Practice Test

Directions: Choose the best answer and fill in the circle of your choice.

1. What is the meaning of the word *bilingual* as it is used in the third paragraph of the selection?

   (A) becoming a serious collector

   (B) being able to read two languages

   (C) being able to exchange one thing for another

   (D) having two options

2. When the author states, "Collecting has become an American craze. People from coast to coast are involved in some form of it," he is trying to convince the reader that _____.

   (A) people who collect comics are crazy

   (B) some kids choose collecting as a leisure-time activity

   (C) people all over the country are collectors

   (D) collecting is popular only in America

3. Which statement is an opinion presented in the selection?

   (A) Comic magazines combine art with storytelling.

   (B) Comics were introduced in the 1930s.

   (C) Current comics cost between $0.75 and $1.75.

   (D) Comics are the most interesting and entertaining of all collectibles.

4. What should a serious comic-book collector do before starting a collection?

   (A) Read newspaper ads and swap and sell to collectors.

   (B) Invest time learning about comics and reading a variety of them.

   (C) Examine a comic book to determine its condition.

   (D) Be prepared to pay more money for older, limited issues of comics.

5. What is the meaning of the word *taste* in the second paragraph of the selection?

   (A) to use a spoon to get the flavor of

   (B) to take a tiny bit of food

   (C) a fondness or liking

   (D) a small quantity or sample of

6. Which statement expresses the author's point of view in the selection?

   (A) Whatever your reason for collecting comics, it is always an enjoyable experience.

   (B) Since you invest both time and money in comic-book collecting, you should make a profit.

   (C) It is definitely more fun to trade comics than to sell them.

   (D) There is no entertainment value to comic-book collecting.

Reading

7. Where are some good places to find new comic books?

a. _____

b. _____

c. _____

8. Where are some good places to find rare and used comic books?

a. _____

b. _____

c. _____

9. Would comic-book collecting be an interesting hobby for you? Explain why or why not.

_____

_____

_____

_____

_____

_____

_____

_____

_____

_____

STOP

Name_____

Directions: Follow along while this selection is read aloud to you.

Creative Money-Making Ideas Pay Off

Michele had to find a way to make some money. This summer, the school chorus members were taking a trip to the shore, and she didn't want to miss it. Everyone had worked hard all year to make enough money to pay for transportation, lodging, and meals. The chorus had held three car washes, two bake sales, a pet wash, and an outdoor concert.

Now that the chorus had enough money for the trip, each member had to come up with his or her own spending money. Michele figured that she would need about $100 for the five-day stay. That would cover souvenirs and still allow her to play miniature golf and rent a bicycle.

Since it was already April, Michele didn't have much time left. The trip was scheduled for June. First, Michele checked with her family to see if there were any extra chores that she could do around the house. Her mom suggested Michele clean the garage. That Saturday, Michele began moving some things out of the garage so she could sweep it and put things in order.

This gave her the idea to have a garage sale. She looked around and found some of her old toys. Her mother and two brothers gave her some things to sell. She made posters to let everyone know when the sale would be held. Then she put the signs up all around her neighborhood and in town. The day of the sale was a bright, sunny day. The sale was a big success.

Michele's next money-making idea was baby-sitting. However, she could only do that on Friday and Saturday nights because she was busy after school on most days. After two weekends of baby-sitting the Costin twins, she had had enough. She had never seen two more active youngsters.

By Memorial Day, Michele decided to see how much money she had saved. Her mom suggested she open a savings account at the bank so she could make some interest on the money and keep it in a safe place. Together they went to the bank, and Michele opened a savings account.

Pre-writing

You will use the ideas from the selection to help you complete two writing activities. For the first activity, you will write a report about the advantages and disadvantages of baby-sitting. For the second activity, you will write an advice column about how to save money.

Directions: The web diagram will help you organize the ideas from the passage in order to write your report. List the advantages and disadvantages of baby-sitting in the spaces below. Then form a conclusion based on a comparison of the two lists.

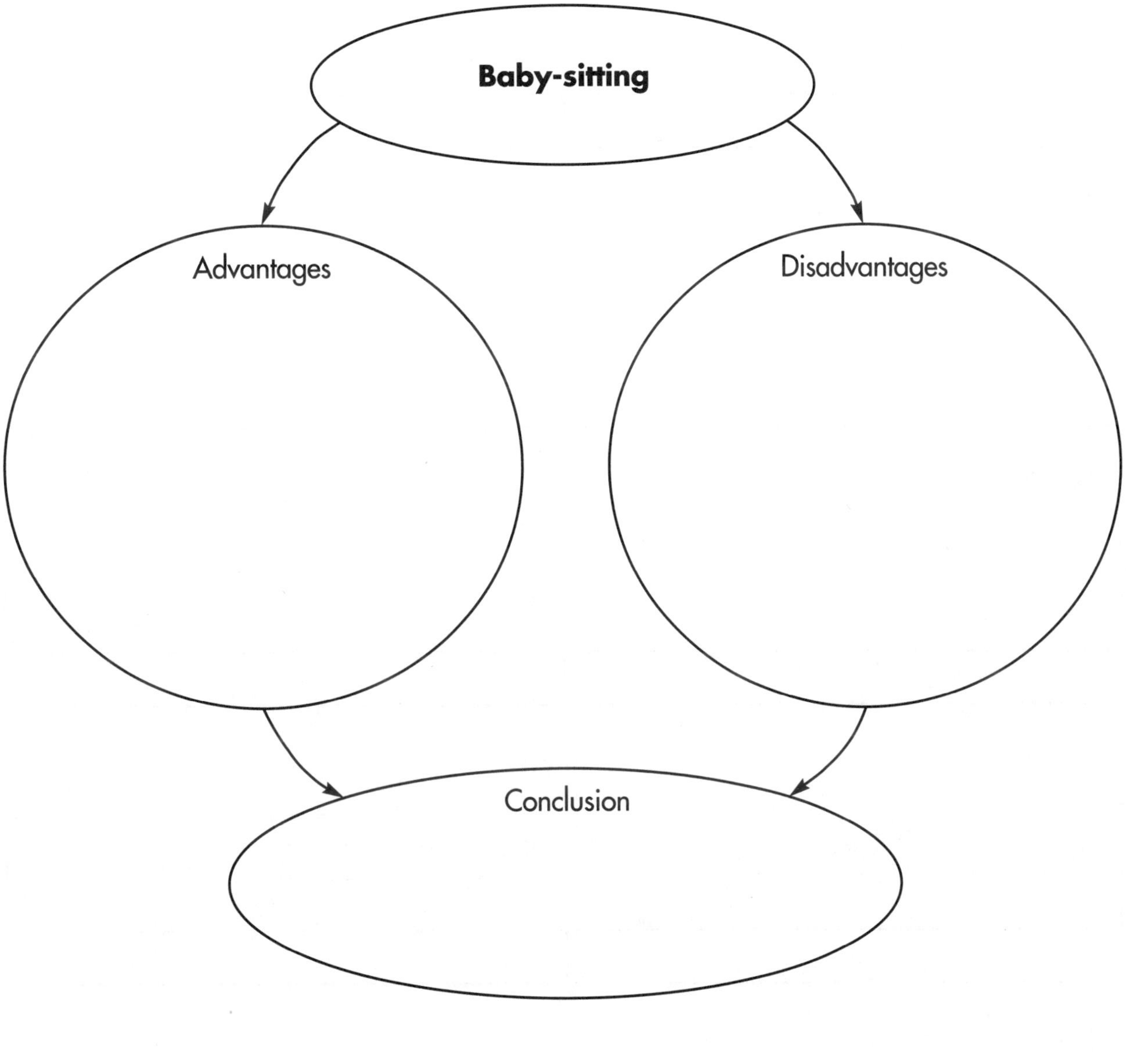

Baby-sitting

Advantages

Disadvantages

Conclusion

© Harcourt

Writing

Name _____

Pre-writing

Directions: Use the flowchart to organize the steps that a person might follow in order to save money.

In order to save money, you will need:

- _____

- _____

- _____

Step 1:

Step 2:

Step 3:

Step 4:

© Harcourt

Report

Directions: For this exercise, you will write a report about the advantages and disadvantages of baby-sitting. You may use the ideas that you wrote on the previous pages. Include at least two advantages and disadvantages. Be sure to include the most important ideas. Use words that make your meanings clear. Be sure that your report is well organized and complete.

Look at the box below. The checklist shows what your writing must have to receive your best score.

Checklist

I will earn my best score if:

⇨ My report explains at least two advantages and two disadvantages of baby-sitting.

⇨ My report includes a topic sentence that tells the main point of the report.

⇨ My report includes details and examples that support the topic sentence.

⇨ My report is well organized and complete.

⇨ I use a variety of words and sentence patterns in my report, and I do not use the same words over and over.

⇨ I spell words correctly.

⇨ I use correct punctuation and capitalization.

Writing

Advice Column

Directions: For this exercise, you will write an advice column about ways to save money. You may use the ideas from the flowchart that you completed. Be sure to give your advice in steps. Be sure to use words that make your directions clear.

Look at the box below. The checklist shows what your writing must have to receive your best score.

Checklist

I will earn my best score if:

⇨ My advice explains how to save money.

⇨ My advice includes step-by-step instructions for how to save money.

⇨ My advice is clear.

⇨ The steps of my advice are given in the correct order.

⇨ My advice column is well organized and complete.

⇨ I use words that make my meaning clear in my advice column, and I do not use the same words over and over.

⇨ I spell words correctly.

⇨ I use correct punctuation and capitalization.

Reading

Directions: Read the selection and answer the questions.

The idea began with a gift Jill had received, the *Guinness Book of World Records*. She began reading the book and became absorbed by the records involving the natural world, the universe, sports, and people's activities of all kinds. Jill shared the information with her friends. Sue thought the item about the $5 million gold bathtub was extraordinary. Beth found it unbelievable that the longest game in baseball's history lasted thirty-three innings.

One morning Jill, Beth, and Sue were quizzing each other about world record trivia. Sue suggested that it would be fun to try to set a Guinness record. The girls laughed, but they agreed that it would be a challenge. They began to think of records set that they might attempt to break. Beth mentioned the record for crawling that had been set in 1987 by two boys who crawled 28 miles. Sue looked up the record for the tallest sand castle. It was five stories high and took 2,000 people to build! Then Jill had a thought. She had often made strings of popcorn to feed to the birds. Why not try to make the world's longest string of popcorn?

For the remainder of the day, the friends made plans. They finally parted, enthusiastic about establishing a new world record.

Over the next month, the friends' weekend mornings were filled with popping popcorn. The afternoons, spent in Jill's garage, were devoted to stringing the kernels. At times, the project became tedious. Sue complained that it was boring; Beth said she detested the smell of popcorn. Jill listened, silently agreeing.

Finally, one Saturday morning, the girls finished stringing the 5,280 feet of popcorn. Then they called their families to share in the proud moment.

That night, Jill slept soundly. The next morning, she heard a clatter and noticed that the garage door was open. As she walked to the garage, the noise became recognizable—it was the sound of squawking birds. When she looked in, she saw the flock nibbling the popcorn. All that remained was a portion of the record-setting popcorn string. Jill was upset. She knew she was the one who had left the door open. All she could do now was shoo the birds away and call Beth and Sue.

When Beth and Sue saw the bits of popcorn and the lengths of exposed string, they knew their dream was gone. Jill apologized and blamed herself. After a while, the girls began talking about the experience of trying to set a world record. They were saddened by the missed opportunity, but they knew they had learned the importance of setting a goal and earnestly trying to achieve it. In their own minds they had set a world record—even if their feat would never make it into the *Guinness Book of World Records.*

Name _____

Constructing Meaning

1. When you started reading the selection, did you think the girls would set a world record? Why or why not?

_____

_____

_____

_____

2. Use the flowchart to record the events of the selection in order.

```
┌─────────────────────────────────────────────┐
│ a. Characters:                                │
│                                               │
└─────────────────────────────────────────────┘
                        ▼
┌─────────────────────────────────────────────┐
│ b. Setting:                                   │
│                                               │
└─────────────────────────────────────────────┘
                        ▼
┌─────────────────────────────────────────────┐
│ c. First Event:                               │
│                                               │
└─────────────────────────────────────────────┘
                        ▼
┌─────────────────────────────────────────────┐
│ d. Second Event:                              │
│                                               │
└─────────────────────────────────────────────┘
                        ▼
┌─────────────────────────────────────────────┐
│ e. Third Event:                               │
│                                               │
└─────────────────────────────────────────────┘
                        ▼
┌─────────────────────────────────────────────┐
│ f. Ending:                                    │
│                                               │
└─────────────────────────────────────────────┘
```

© Harcourt

Reading

Extending Meaning

1. Do you think Jill, Beth, and Sue will try again to set a world record? Explain your answer.

_____

_____

_____

_____

_____

_____

_____

_____

2. What is the author's purpose in writing this selection? Support your answer with information from the text.

_____

_____

_____

_____

_____

_____

_____

_____

Practice Test

Directions: Choose the best answer and fill in the circle of your choice.

1. What is the meaning of the word *trivia* as it is used in the first sentence of the second paragraph of the selection?

   (A) important matters or facts

   (B) interesting or entertaining facts

   (C) interesting jokes

   (D) exaggerated statements

2. Which of these events occurred last in the selection?

   (A) Jill received an edition of the *Guinness Book of World Records* as a present.

   (B) Jill, Beth, and Sue decided to try to set a Guinness world record.

   (C) The birds ate the popcorn from the record-setting popcorn string.

   (D) The girls told their families that they had finished making the popcorn string.

3. What was the most important effect of Jill's leaving the garage door open?

   (A) Jill had to call Sue and Beth to explain what had happened.

   (B) Jill had to shoo the birds out of her garage.

   (C) The birds nibbled on the popcorn.

   (D) The girls lost their opportunity to set a Guinness world record.

4. You can tell from this selection that the *Guinness Book of World Records* _____.

   (A) is a book that both adults and young people enjoy reading

   (B) contains many facts about world records that are entertaining to read about

   (C) has information about records set by the animal kingdom

   (D) is a book that is in every library's collection

5. How do you think Jill felt when she realized that she was responsible for leaving the garage door open?

   (A) disappointed in herself

   (B) angry with Beth and Sue

   (C) amazed by the situation

   (D) determined to be more responsible

6. What is the setting for most of this selection?

   (A) a mechanic's garage in the fall months

   (B) several mornings at school

   (C) many weekends in Jill's garage

   (D) Beth's kitchen on Saturday mornings

© Harcourt

GO ON

Name _____

7. Choose one of the following words that you think best describes the girls' attitude about trying to set a world record: *determined, worried, afraid.* Explain your answer.

_____

_____

_____

_____

_____

_____

_____

_____

_____

_____

8. What did the girls learn about setting goals?

_____

_____

_____

_____

_____

_____

_____

_____

_____

_____

© Harcourt

STOP

Reading

Name _____

Directions: Read the selection and answer the questions.

The ancient Mayas, a native people of the Americas, left written records that historians are now finally learning to read. For a long time, these pictures and symbols were mysteries to us. Now that present-day students of Mayan culture have begun to figure out and read the hieroglyphics, much about this great culture has come to be known.

The early Mayas, who were spread across Mesoamerica in what is now Mexico, Belize, Honduras, and Guatemala, had an advanced calendar system. Calendars noted the passing of the seasons and the cycles of floods. They also showed the solar and lunar years and the positions of the planets.

Historians had long believed that the Mayas were interested mainly in keeping track of planting and harvesting times and watching the skies.

The Mayan records that twentieth-century historians first learned to read were calendars that kept a "long count," or a precise record of days that started from a date of zero. Day zero on the Mayan calendar was August 10, 3113 B.C. These findings provided historians with more information about how the Mayas kept track of time.

When experts learned to read more of the hieroglyphics, they were able to get a fuller picture of early Mayan culture. From about the third century A.D., the Mayas began to write other historical records on hard materials such as bone, pottery, and walls. These writings tell of the key events in the lives of their rulers and show how important the kings and queens were to the people. The Mayas also recorded their own history, religious beliefs, and myths in these writings.

The Mayas kept careful records of what happened in their times. In fact, they were the first people in the Western Hemisphere to create an advanced writing system. This system is the only true pre-Columbian writing system.

Constructing Meaning

1. **While reading, you may have seen some words that were unfamiliar to you. If you used other parts of the selection to figure out what the words meant, then you used context clues. Read these sentences and use prior knowledge or context clues to figure out what the words mean. Then write the underlined words in a sentence of your own.**

   a. For a long time, pictures and symbols called <u>hieroglyphics</u> could not be read by those studying Mayan culture.

   _____

   _____

   b. <u>Mesoamerica</u>, in what is now Mexico, Belize, Honduras, and Guatemala, was home to early Mayas.

   _____

   _____

2. **Fill in the word web with words from the selection that are related to the word *hieroglyphics*.**

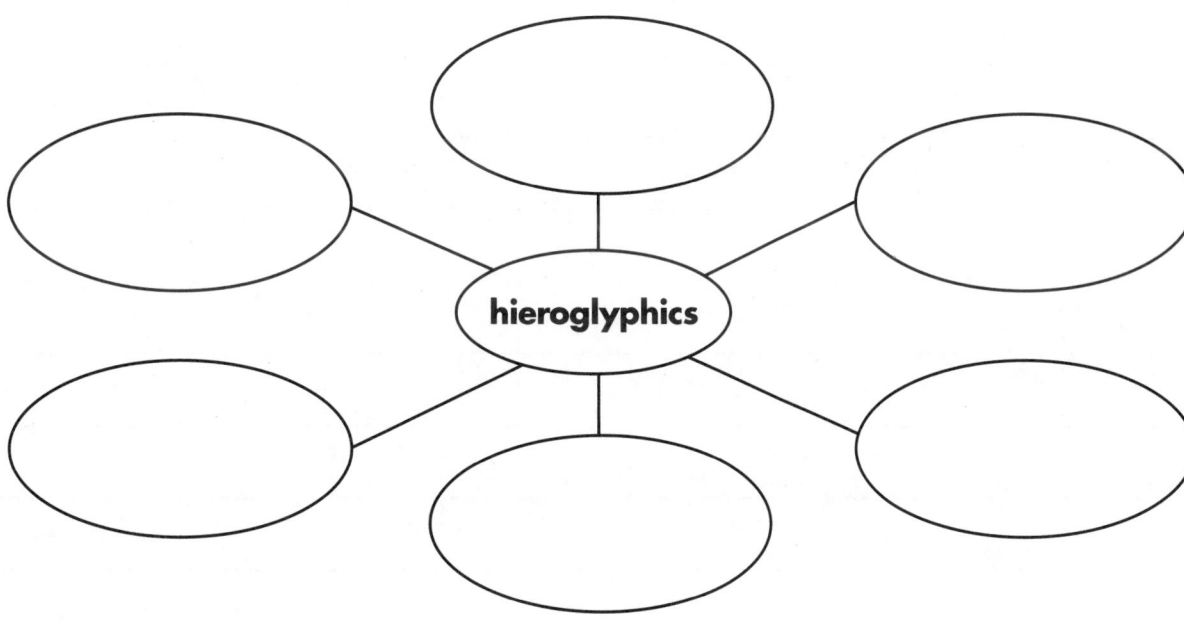

Extending Meaning

1. In which of the following sources could you find more information about the kings and queens of the Mayan people: *The Rulers of the Mayas* or *A History of Hieroglyphics*? Support your answer.

_____

_____

_____

_____

_____

_____

_____

2. Would you recommend this selection to a friend? Why or why not?

_____

_____

_____

_____

_____

_____

_____

_____

Name _____

Reading

Practice Test

Directions: Choose the best answer and fill in the circle of your choice.

1. Which of these is the best summary for this selection?

   Ⓐ Historians need to study a people's language for many years.

   Ⓑ Historians have found that Mayan hieroglyphics are hard to read.

   Ⓒ The Mayas kept exact calendars that recorded the passage of time.

   Ⓓ As historians learn to read Mayan records, they gain a more accurate picture of Mayan culture.

2. What is the meaning of the word *hieroglyphics* as it is used in the first paragraph of the selection?

   Ⓐ a method of creating lunar calendars

   Ⓑ a writing system of pictures and symbols

   Ⓒ a record of seasonal floods

   Ⓓ a mythology of important heroes

3. What is the meaning of the word *Mesoamerica* as it is used in the second paragraph of the selection?

   Ⓐ the Midwestern United States

   Ⓑ an area in Columbia

   Ⓒ the countries now called Mexico, Belize, Honduras, and Guatemala

   Ⓓ Costa Rica, Brazil, and Argentina

4. Why did the Mayas have a calendar that kept a precise record of days?

   Ⓐ to keep track of solar and lunar years

   Ⓑ to keep track of planting and harvesting time and to watch the sky

   Ⓒ to keep track of ceremonies

   Ⓓ to keep track of their writing system

5. Which of these is a fact presented in the selection?

   Ⓐ The Mayas practiced rituals.

   Ⓑ Mayan religious beliefs were different from those of modern people.

   Ⓒ Mayan writings showed how important the kings and queens were.

   Ⓓ Mayan mythology is more interesting than Greek mythology.

6. You can tell from this selection that

   _____.

   Ⓐ historians must spend many years studying written records before they truly understand a culture

   Ⓑ the first scholars were not good students of language

   Ⓒ historians will never understand the Mayan calendar

   Ⓓ historians will never be able to read Mayan hieroglyphics

© Harcourt

GO ON

7. List three things mentioned in this article that historians discovered about the Mayan people.

a. _____

b. _____

c. _____

8. What did the Mayas record about their culture by using hieroglyphics?

_____

_____

_____

9. What was the most interesting fact that you learned from reading this article? Explain why.

_____

_____

_____

_____

_____

_____

_____

_____

STOP

Name _____

Directions: Follow along while this selection is read aloud to you.

Just Going Fishing

I always thought of fishing as a simple pleasure. You got your fishing pole, took your bait, and went to the water. However, I learned just how complicated a fishing trip can be when I went with my grandfather and Uncle Barry.

Last Friday afternoon, Grandfather suggested we take his boat out to the Gulf of Mexico for a fishing trip the next day. Uncle Barry and I immediately said yes.

"Good, let's get started," Grandfather said.

"Get started!" I said. "We're going out tomorrow! Not today, right?"

"Yes, but there's a lot to be done and we'll want to leave here at daybreak tomorrow," Grandfather said.

I looked at Uncle Barry, and he was smiling with a "you haven't seen anything yet" look on his face.

I was game, though. I mean, how difficult could it be to go fishing? "Okay, what do we do first?" I asked.

"First we'll call the weather station for tomorrow's weather and tide forecast. Then if it looks good for tomorrow, we'll check the rods and reels," Grandfather began. "After that we'll get some ice and food supplies and prepare the food."

The weather report predicted clear and sunny weather for the next day, and the tides were right for a good day of fishing, Grandfather reported.

"Why, I know a spot that is just jumping with fat grouper," he told us.

Then we checked the rods and reels. We were going to use heavier rods and fishing line because of the size and type of fish we were going to catch. We would use bigger hooks, too.

As Grandfather mapped out a course for us to follow on a sea chart, Uncle Barry and I were busy preparing sandwiches and snacks. Grandfather reminded us to pack some canned meats and a large container of fresh water. He reminded us of a time he had been stranded for two days because of boat trouble and how relieved he had been to have those emergency rations and water.

"Okay, now that we have our forecast, the food, the water, the fishing gear, and our maps (one for us and one to leave with Grandmother so someone will know our whereabouts), let's go check out the boat," Grandfather said.

We filled the gas tanks and checked the battery, the horn, the lights, the life vests, and the emergency kit. By now I was beginning to think fishing was just a lot of hard work. When did the fun start?

Saturday came and the daylight barely warmed the refreshing cool morning air. Grandfather set the instruments with the proper coordinates he had mapped out so the boat would follow the course to his favorite fishing spot. It took us nearly an hour to get there, but it was worth it. Not long after we set our lines, Grandfather and I both pulled in two big groupers. Now that is what fishing is all about!

Name _____

Pre-writing

You will use the ideas from the selection to help you complete two writing activities. For the first activity, you will write instructions for how to plan a trip. For the second activity, you will write a report about a trip you have taken.

Directions: The story map below will help you identify important information about planning a trip. Fill in the circles with words, ideas, and information from the passage "Just Going Fishing" that relate to trip-planning.

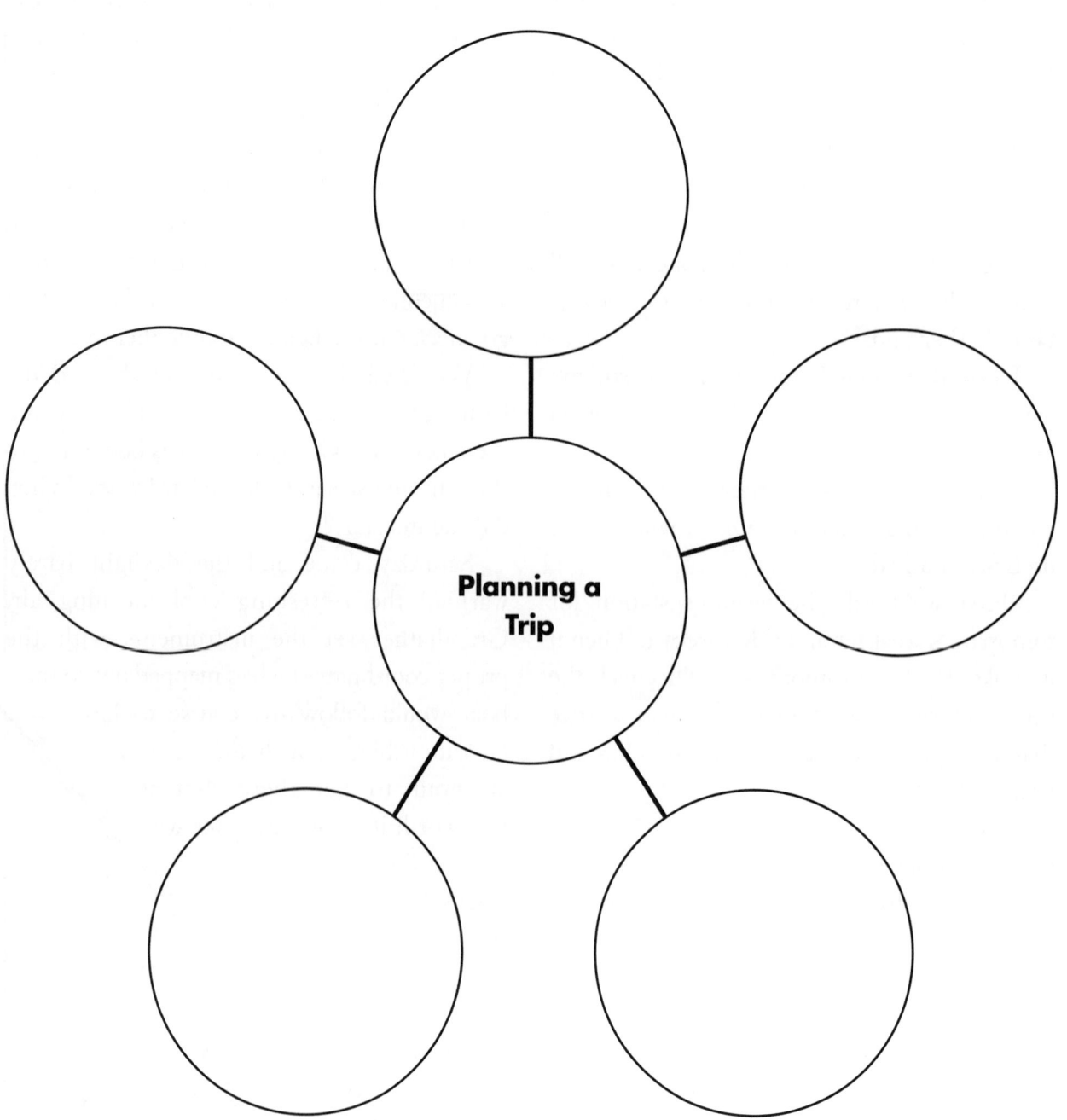

Planning a Trip

Pre-writing

Directions: Use the diagram to organize information about a trip you have taken. (Your trip does not have to be a long vacation. It can be a school trip or a trip to the grocery store.)

On my trip, I went to

_____

What I **Did**

-
-
-

What I **Saw**

-
-
-

What I **Learned**

-
-
-

Writing

Instructions

Directions: For this exercise, you will write instructions on how to plan a trip. You may use the ideas that you wrote on previous pages. Be sure to give the instructions in steps. Also, be sure that you give the steps in a logical order. Use words that make your instructions clear.

Look at the box below. The checklist shows what your writing must have to receive your best score.

Checklist

I will earn my best score if:

⇨ My instructions explain how to plan a trip.

⇨ My instructions are clear.

⇨ My instructions are given in steps.

⇨ The steps in my instructions are given in the correct order.

⇨ My instructions are well organized and complete.

⇨ I use words in my instructions that make my meaning clear, and I do not use the same words over and over.

⇨ I spell words correctly.

⇨ I use correct punctuation and capitalization.

© Harcourt

Name _____

Report

Directions: For this exercise, you will write a report about a trip that you have taken. You may use ideas from the story map you completed. Be sure to mention where you went, one thing you did, one thing you saw, and one thing you learned.

Look at the box below. The checklist shows what your writing must have to receive your best score.

Checklist

I will earn my best score if:

⇨ My report includes a topic sentence that identifies my trip.

⇨ My report explains one thing that I did.

⇨ My report explains one thing that I saw.

⇨ My report explains one thing that I learned on my trip.

⇨ My report is well organized and complete.

⇨ I use a variety of words and sentence patterns in my report, and I do not use the same words over and over.

⇨ I spell words correctly.

⇨ I use correct punctuation and capitalization.

Directions: Read the selection and answer the questions.

Do you like kittens? Meet Tike and Tabby, young felines who were abandoned alongside a busy street. Thanks to the perseverance of two teens, the kittens are now safe. Unfortunately, the teens are unable to keep these adorable kittens. Tike and Tabby are two of the hundreds of abandoned kittens in our area shelters that need loving homes. This is their story.

About a month ago, Chris noticed a kitten at the back door of the restaurant where his sister Jody works. Curious, he got out of the car and followed it. It scurried across the parking lot and then down a steep embankment to a clump of trees and rocks below. Then Chris discovered that there was a second kitten. Both animals were scrawny and appeared to be terrified of him. His heart went out to the kittens because he knew they must be very hungry. He had to do something.

Chris's sister wouldn't be finished for another ten minutes, so he drove to the supermarket and purchased some cat food. Putting the opened cans where they could be easily seen by the kittens, he waited. Within minutes the hungry animals scrambled up the side of the hill and devoured the food. But as Chris approached them, they ran off. They were apparently unaccustomed to people. By that time, all the restaurant's employees had come out. Chris asked about the kittens. One person said she had seen them. Another explained how a customer had almost hit a kitten in the parking lot. However, no one had done anything to help the abandoned animals.

Over the next few days, Chris and Jody made a series of phone calls to various animal organizations in the area. An animal shelter in the area was already overcrowded and could take no more kittens. A shelter in another community was willing to take the kittens for a fee. There weren't too many options for these animals.

Each day for the next month, Chris or Jody stopped to feed the kittens, hoping to get closer to them. Gradually, the animals seemed to recognize the teens and appeared to be less apprehensive. By the end of the second week, the kittens would run up the hill when they realized the teens were there. Finally, two weeks later, Chris and Jody were able to touch the kittens. Then they managed to coax the animals into a carrier.

Tike and Tabby are now at Cat's Meow Shelter waiting for someone like you. For a fee of $20, you can adopt one of these loving animals. This fee pays for your new pet's vaccinations and medical care.

Chris and Jody are now volunteers at the shelter. If you would like to become a volunteer, adopt a kitten, or make a donation, please call 555-1345. Cat's Meow also offers a film about animal care.

Name _____

Constructing Meaning

1. **Tell how the author describes the kittens in the selection.**

_____

_____

_____

_____

_____

_____

_____

_____

2. **Write a brief summary of the selection. Remember that when you summarize, you tell a shortened version of the original text in your own words. You should give only the most important information from the selection.**

_____

_____

_____

_____

_____

_____

_____

_____

Extending Meaning

1. **Do you think Chris and Jody are glad that they helped the kittens? Why or why not?**

   _____

   _____

   _____

   _____

2. **Would you recommend this selection to a friend? Why or why not?**

   _____

   _____

   _____

   _____

3. **Use the Venn diagram to compare the similarities and differences of two kinds of pets that you would like to have.**

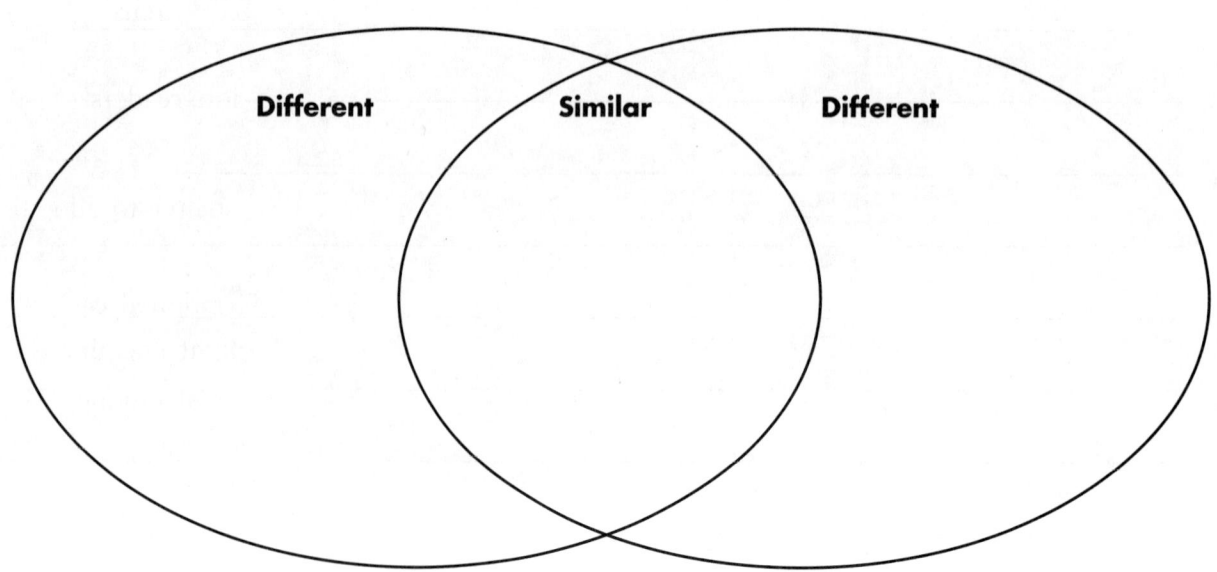

Different   **Similar**   **Different**

© Harcourt

Practice Test

Directions: Choose the best answer and fill in the circle of your choice.

1. What is the meaning of the word *unaccustomed* as it is used in the third paragraph of the selection?

   (A) completely used to

   (B) not used to

   (C) somewhat used to

   (D) not a customer

2. When the author states, "Tike and Tabby are two of the hundreds of abandoned kittens in our area shelters that need loving homes," he or she is trying to convince the reader _____.

   (A) that cats make excellent pets

   (B) that animal shelters take good care of abandoned cats

   (C) that Tike and Tabby are lucky to have been adopted

   (D) to consider adopting an abandoned cat or kitten

3. From time to time, trying and failing to catch the two kittens probably made the teens feel _____.

   (A) frustrated

   (B) ridiculous

   (C) proud

   (D) impatient

4. The teens tried to catch the kittens themselves because _____.

   (A) they wanted the kittens as pets

   (B) the shelters were overcrowded

   (C) they saw no other option

   (D) they liked cats

5. Which of the following is the best summary of this selection?

   (A) Tabby and Tike, two kittens, are abandoned by two teens.

   (B) Two teens ask the public to open their homes to abandoned kittens.

   (C) Kittens can be adopted for a fee of $20, which will cover the cost of shots.

   (D) Through the efforts of two teens, the public is made aware of the plight of abandoned kittens.

6. After reading this selection, readers might _____.

   (A) go to the nearest shelter to adopt a kitten

   (B) try to help any abandoned cats they themselves might encounter

   (C) go out and look for abandoned or stray kittens in the area

   (D) all of the above

GO ON

7. Choose one word from the following that you think best describes Chris and Jody's attitude toward the kittens: *uncaring, concerned, sad.* Support your choice with information from the selection.

_____

_____

_____

_____

_____

_____

_____

_____

8. Do you think the author of the selection thinks that helping animals is important? Support your opinion with information from the selection.

_____

_____

_____

_____

_____

_____

_____

_____

STOP

Directions: Read the selection and answer the questions.

In the Middle Ages in Europe, only a few people knew how to read and write. Before the thirteenth century, most books in Europe were produced by monks, scribes, and skilled illustrators. Each copy had to be handwritten by scribes. In the fourteenth century, books were made and enjoyed mostly at universities, which were accessible only to a privileged class. By the fifteenth century, there existed a large reading public, hungry for printed material. Yet books were still expensive to produce and difficult to get.

This problem was solved by the development of movable type. Around 1450, a German craftsman and inventor named Johannes Gutenberg worked to create a printing press that could produce unlimited copies of any book. Gutenberg's press worked on the principle of replica-casting. With replica-casting, individual letters were engraved and stamped into brass. Copies of the type could then be cast from metal. When the replicas, or copies, were put together, they made a flat printing surface. The screw-and-lever press that Gutenberg designed could print an entire page at a time, as well as many copies of the same page. He also experimented with inks until he came up with a kind that stuck to the metal type.

This printing press began a revolution in the printing industry in Europe. Venice became the great center of the printing trade. Following Gutenberg's lead, other crafts workers, including Nicolas Jenson, Aldus Manutius, and William Caxton, learned the art of printing handsome and affordable books. Although early books looked much like the older manuscripts, printers soon began to make books that looked more modern. These books even carried copyright details.

Gutenberg's press helped bring about a new era of communications. News, ideas, and art traveled much more rapidly. As reading material became cheaper and easier to obtain, the public became more informed about the world.

Constructing Meaning

1. **List five of the benefits of the Gutenberg movable-type printing press.**

   a. _____

   b. _____

   c. _____

   d. _____

   e. _____

2. **Which of the facts in the selection did you find most unusual or interesting? Explain your answer.**

   _____

   _____

   _____

   _____

   _____

   _____

   _____

   _____

   _____

   _____

   _____

   _____

Name _____

Extending Meaning

1. **If you wanted to research additional information about the Gutenberg printing press, which of the sources below would you use to find the best information? Support your answer.**
   encyclopedia
   dictionary
   a current newspaper article
   thesaurus

   _____

   _____

   _____

   _____

   _____

   _____

2. **Use the chart to compare and contrast the printing process before the movable-type printing press and after its invention.**

Before	**After**

© Harcourt

Practice Test

1. Which of these is the best summary for this selection?

(A) Gutenberg was an inventor.

(B) The Gutenberg press helped people get books and brought about a new era of communication.

(C) The first typeset books looked like hand-copied manuscripts.

(D) During the fifteenth century, books were kept by scholars.

2. Before the invention of the Gutenberg press, books were difficult for Europeans to obtain, mainly because _____.

(A) the amount of labor needed to produce a book meant that few books were available

(B) the prices of books were so high that few people could buy them

(C) books were usually produced in places far from Europe

(D) libraries had not been established

3. What is the meaning of the term *movable type* as it is used in the second paragraph of the selection?

(A) lightweight books that could be carried easily

(B) type that is cut by hand, one letter at a time

(C) a portable printing press that can fit on a desktop

(D) letters and numbers made from pieces of metal that can be placed in any order to form words

4. What is the meaning of the word *unlimited* as it is used in the second paragraph of the selection?

(A) of poor quality

(B) without page numbers

(C) without end, boundless

(D) without mistakes

5. Gutenberg's printing press saved hours of the printer's labor because _____.

(A) it was operated by electric power

(B) it was fully computerized

(C) it could print a whole page at one time and make many copies

(D) it did not require an experienced person to run it

6. The selection gives you enough information to conclude that _____.

(A) when books are available, everyone will learn to read

(B) people were ignorant in the days before Gutenberg's press

(C) it doesn't matter what people read

(D) the printed word is a powerful educational tool

© Harcourt

GO ON

7. How were most books produced in Europe before the thirteenth century?

_____

_____

_____

_____

_____

_____

8. List three people mentioned in the selection (other than Gutenberg) who were involved in printing affordable books.

    a. _____

    b. _____

    c. _____

9. What is replica-casting? Use information from the story to support your answer.

_____

_____

_____

_____

_____

_____

_____

_____

_____

_____

STOP

Name _____

Directions: Follow along while this selection is read aloud to you.

Why Should We Recycle?

Fellow Students:

I have been given permission to speak to you about a new project. A number of us are interested in starting a student-operated recycling center. We met with the principal, Ms. Black, to discuss the idea, and she was encouraging. She said we can use part of the school basement for our recycling center. She will allow us to begin this effort, however, only if the whole student body is behind the center, which means we need lots of volunteers and moral support.

Many of you are probably wondering, "Why do we need a recycling center? What will volunteering do for me?"

Let's face it: Whoever we are, and whatever our interests, we are all living on the same planet. We all depend on the health of our air, trees, and water. This is what a recycling center is all about. Every time new paper is made, trees must be cut down, and when we lose trees, we lose helpers in the fight against air pollution.

Just think about how much we throw out and how much land we use to dump our garbage. The earth isn't growing; there is less and less land to fill up with garbage. What will happen in the future? We have to think about the kids who will be here after we are gone— *our* kids!

If we recycle things instead of throwing them out, we meet two important goals. First, we need fewer new raw materials, such as wood, soil, fresh water, oil, and coal. Second, we have less garbage to throw away. There are other benefits—personal benefits. If we get in the habit of recycling, we'll begin to take responsibility for the world. This will help us become mature adults.

Since we use so much paper in school, the chief goal of the recycling center will be to collect used paper products. We will separate white, colored, and glossy paper. Then we will sell the paper to a recycling factory. The factory will provide the transportation. Here is where we need volunteers. Some people are needed to set up paper-collection boxes in each classroom and to bring these down to the center when they are filled. We need other people to collect paper around the community and bring it to the recycling center. The volunteer sign-up list is in the gym.

As you consider your decision, remember two things. First, if we collect enough paper, we may make enough money for an end-of-the-year field trip to the aquarium or to Forest Park. Second, if we do not get enough signatures, there will be no school recycling center, even though the health of our environment depends on each one of us. I know that each student will try to meet this challenge. Thank you.

Name _____

Pre-writing

You will use the ideas from the selection to help you complete two writing activities. For the first activity, you will write an essay that identifies a problem at your school and offers a solution. For the second activity, you will write a letter to the editor that explains the benefits of volunteering in your community.

Directions: Use the chart below to organize your ideas about a problem at school and its solution. Fill in the parts of the chart with information, words, or ideas from the passage "Why Should We Recycle?"

Problem:

Solution 1

Solution 2

Which solution works better? Why? _____

_____

_____

Writing

Pre-writing

Directions: Answer the questions and fill in the outline to organize your letter to the editor about the benefits of volunteering.

What are the benefits of volunteering?	Why should people volunteer?
Benefit 1: _____ _____	Reason 1: _____ _____
Benefit 2: _____ _____	Reason 2: _____ _____
Benefit 3: _____ _____	Reason 3: _____ _____

(Date) _____

(Greeting) Dear Editor:

(Body) There are many benefits to volunteering in the community. They include

_____, _____,

and _____.

There are several reasons we should volunteer in the community. One reason is

_____.

Another reason is _____.

A final reason is _____.

(Closing) Sincerely,

(Signature) _____

© Harcourt

Name _____

Writing

Problem-Solution Essay

Directions: For this exercise, you will write about a problem at your school and offer a solution. You may use the ideas from the chart you completed. Remember that you should state the problem clearly and offer two possible solutions. Finally, you should explain which solution works better. Be sure to provide reasons for your ideas.

Look at the box below. The checklist shows what your writing must have to receive your best score.

Checklist

I will earn my best score if:

⇨ My paper clearly identifies a problem.

⇨ My paper clearly identifies two solutions.

⇨ My paper tells which solution is better and why.

⇨ My paper provides good reasons to support my ideas.

⇨ My paper is well organized and complete.

⇨ I use words to make my meaning clear in my paper, and I do not use the same words over and over.

⇨ I spell words correctly.

⇨ I use correct punctuation and capitalization.

© Harcourt

Writing

Letter to the Editor

Directions: For this exercise, you will write a letter to the editor that explains the benefits of volunteering. You may use the ideas you wrote in the charts on the previous pages. Be sure to state at least three benefits of volunteering. Also, be sure to include reasons that support your ideas. Be sure to use the format for a letter—including the date, a greeting, a body, a closing, and a signature.

Look at the box below. The checklist shows what your writing must have to receive your best score.

Checklist

I will earn my best score if:

➭ My letter includes a greeting, a body, a closing, and a signature.

➭ My letter identifies at least three benefits of volunteering.

➭ My letter contains reasons that support my ideas about volunteering.

➭ My letter is well organized and complete.

➭ In my letter, I use a variety of words and sentence patterns, and I do not use the same words over and over.

➭ I spell words correctly.

➭ I use correct punctuation and capitalization.

© Harcourt

Directions: Read the selection and answer the questions.

"You forgot the freezer bag."

"Huh?"

"The freezer bag for my frozen juice."

"Oh, I'm sorry. Here's one. Have a nice day."

What am I doing working here? I don't even like to shop in this supermarket. The money helps—that's what I said last Friday when I got my check. But this is my second week, and I'm still getting everything wrong. I forget that skim milk costs more than whole milk. I confuse spinach with chard and the large, expensive pink grapefruits with the small, white ones. I mess up the cash register total when I subtract coupons, and the bags I load have a habit of breaking before my customers even leave the store!

It'll get better. That's what Mom tells me. Besides, it's only for three hours every day after school.

Now look who just came into the store! She's wearing sunglasses. Where does she think she is, Miami Beach? You couldn't find the sun today with a telescope and a light meter. She has that look, too. That's one thing I've learned while working here. I can tell who's going to be trouble.

She must expect a food shortage. She is buying everything in the store and walking around like she owns the place.

Here she comes. She can't stuff anything more in her shopping cart.

"I'd like two separate receipts—one for the fruit and vegetables and the other for everything else," she announces.

I knew it. She *would* ask for something difficult like that. I separate the items into two piles and then start entering them into the

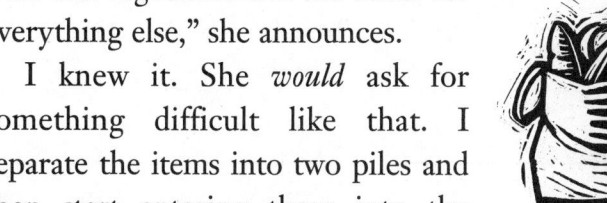

cash register. I'm getting a little faster at this. My fingers don't exactly dance over the register, but they're not limping over it either.

"Here you go, ma'am. Please take your receipts."

She checks them over and then asks, "Did you charge me twice on the soup? There are two grocery items at $1.09, and I only had one can."

"No, ma'am. The other $1.09 is for the mushrooms."

"Oh, how silly of me. You're right. By the way, could I have four quarters back for this single? And the gum, did you pack the gum? I want it for my ride."

"The gum?"

I search through the bags, looking for the gum, and of course, I can't find it until I unpack half of the things.

"Here's your gum, ma'am."

Boy, am I glad she's out the door! I was right. I picked her out as trouble as soon as she came in. She's the type who enjoys giving cashiers a hard time. Oh, no. She's coming back. I must have done something wrong.

"Is the manager here?" she asks.

"He's in the back, ma'am, doing inventory."

Oh, no. What did I do this time?

She's coming toward me with the manager, but now her sunglasses are off. They're coming over to my register.

"Young man," she says, "I'm Juanita Schmidt, the regional manager of this chain of stores. I want to commend you for your excellent and courteous service. You are the employee of the month. Here is a check for one hundred dollars."

Reading

Constructing Meaning

1. Use the flowchart to retell the events that occurred in the selection in order after the customer took off her sunglasses.

EVENTS

a.

b.

c.

d.

2. What is the main idea of this selection? In other words, what point is the author trying to make in this selection?

_____

_____

_____

Extending Meaning

1. Describe the narrator's attitude before the customer revealed her identity.

   _____

   _____

   _____

   _____

   _____

2. How do you think the narrator felt about the customer after she revealed her identity?

   _____

   _____

   _____

   _____

   _____

3. Do you think the narrator is a good employee? Explain why or why not.

   _____

   _____

   _____

   _____

   _____

   _____

Name _____

Practice Test

Directions: Choose the best answer and fill in the circle of your choice.

1. The narrator's attitude toward his job can best be described as _____.

   (A) cheery but careless

   (B) grateful and enthusiastic

   (C) uneasy but hopeful

   (D) boastful and inconsiderate

2. It can be inferred from the story that the regional manager wore sunglasses because _____.

   (A) the sun was bright outside

   (B) the store lights were very strong

   (C) she did not want to be recognized

   (D) sunglasses had been on sale

3. How did the way the narrator actually handled his customer contrast with his earlier description of his abilities?

   (A) He was better than he described himself.

   (B) He was not nearly as good as he thought he was.

   (C) He had clearly forgotten most of what he had learned.

   (D) He was better at finding gum than he described.

4. According to the selection, which of these events occurred after the customer took off her sunglasses?

   (A) She asked for the manager.

   (B) She left the store with the groceries.

   (C) She presented the narrator with a check.

   (D) She asked the narrator to find her gum.

5. Which of these statements expresses the narrator's opinion of the customer?

   (A) She questioned the total on the grocery receipt.

   (B) She entered the store in sunglasses.

   (C) She was out to give him a hard time.

   (D) She was a snoop and a spy.

6. The author probably wrote the selection in order to _____.

   (A) encourage people to become cashiers

   (B) teach people about good super-market manners

   (C) show that life is full of surprises

   (D) show that hard work does not really pay off

© Harcourt

GO ON

Name _____

7. Choose one of the following words that you think best describes the way the narrator treated the customer: *angrily, patiently, unkindly.* Explain your answer.

_____

_____

_____

_____

_____

_____

_____

8. Do you think the narrator deserved to be named employee of the month and awarded the check for one hundred dollars? Explain why or why not.

_____

_____

_____

_____

_____

_____

_____

_____

STOP

Directions: Read the selection and answer the questions.

In November 1989, an event took place in the city of Berlin, Germany, that made world news. The Berlin Wall, for twenty-eight years a symbol of a divided nation, was torn down. People from both East Berlin and West Berlin cheered, cried, and embraced. Some held up pieces of the wall that had long separated them from friends and relatives.

How did a city come to be divided by a wall? The answer lies in the troubled history of post-World War II Europe. When the war ended, the Allies agreed to a division of Germany. The four countries that had led the fight against Hitler in World War II—the United States, Great Britain, France, and the Soviet Union—divided Germany into four occupation zones. The capital, Berlin, which lay in the middle of the Soviet zone, was also divided into four zones. In 1949, the three Western zones of the country were unified, forming the Federal Republic of Germany, a parliamentary democracy. In the Eastern zone, the Soviets created the German Democratic Republic.

The division of its former capital city symbolized the breakup of Germany into the East of communism and the West of democracy. The West German chancellors kept close ties with Western Europe and the United States, while East Germany was controlled by the Soviet bloc. Families and friends were separated as Cold War tensions strained communication between the two nations.

Many East Germans protested against communism. Under this system, industry grew rapidly, but living conditions became worse because the Soviet Union took most of the profits. Meanwhile, the West Germans prospered. In 1961, the Berlin Wall was built to stop the large numbers of East Germans who were trying to escape to West Berlin in search of freedom.

In 1989, major reforms in Hungary, Poland, and the Soviet Union inspired East Germans to flee to the West. Those who did not flee protested. Communism was on the point of collapse, and the Soviets did not come to the aid of the East German government. In November, the Berlin Wall came down. In 1990, Germany was reunified and began working toward economic recovery.

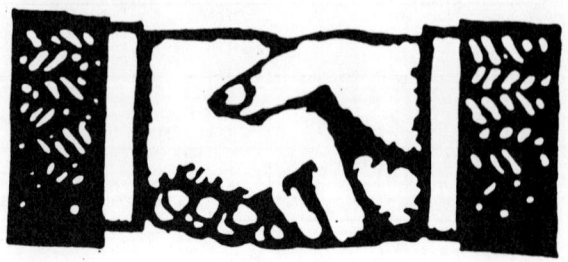

Name _____

Constructing Meaning

1. The author describes the Berlin Wall as "a symbol of a divided nation." What does the author mean by this? Support your answers with information from the selection.

_____

_____

_____

_____

_____

_____

_____

_____

_____

2. According to the selection, how did the city of Berlin come to be divided by a wall? Support your answers with information from the selection.

_____

_____

_____

_____

_____

_____

_____

_____

© Harcourt

Extending Meaning

1. Use information from the selection to fill in the cause-and-effect chart.

Cause:	Effect:
Communism in eastern Europe collapses in 1989.	a.
b.	Germany begins to work toward economic recovery.

2. Would you recommend this selection to a friend doing a research paper on Germany? Why or why not?

_____

_____

_____

_____

_____

_____

_____

Practice Test

Directions: Choose the best answer and fill in the circle of your choice.

1. Which of these is the best summary for this selection?

   Ⓐ The Allies won World War II.

   Ⓑ East Germany's economy was ruined by communism.

   Ⓒ The tearing down of the Berlin Wall symbolized the changing political situation in Germany.

   Ⓓ Berlin prospered under democracy.

2. Why were East and West Berliners happy when the Berlin Wall came down?

   Ⓐ They wanted Berlin to be divided.

   Ⓑ It meant their nation would no longer be divided.

   Ⓒ The people wanted communism and democracy.

   Ⓓ Communism had been difficult.

3. What is the meaning of the word *Allies* as it is used in the second paragraph of the selection?

   Ⓐ supporters of the German Democratic Republic

   Ⓑ West German chancellors

   Ⓒ the nations that led the fight against Hitler during World War II

   Ⓓ East Germans who did not like the current political situation

4. The city of Berlin was originally divided because _____.

   Ⓐ many German people wanted to support communism

   Ⓑ it was the former German capital

   Ⓒ the East Germans and the West Germans did not want to see each other

   Ⓓ there was no good system of transportation

5. Conditions became worse in East Germany during Soviet control because _____.

   Ⓐ the people did not have jobs

   Ⓑ the people could not go to West Germany

   Ⓒ the Soviet Union took most of the profits from industry

   Ⓓ families and friends were separated

6. Which of these probably best describes many East Germans in the years leading up to the tearing down of the Berlin Wall?

   Ⓐ happy and financially well-off

   Ⓑ satisfied with their political leaders

   Ⓒ grateful for Soviet control

   Ⓓ angry about their government and about the failing economy

© Harcourt

GO ON

7. What happened in Germany after Berlin was divided?

_____

_____

_____

_____

_____

_____

_____

_____

8. According to the selection, why was the Berlin Wall constructed?

_____

_____

_____

_____

_____

9. List three things mentioned in the selection that the people of East and West Berlin did when the Berlin Wall was torn down.

a. _____

b. _____

c. _____

STOP

Directions: Follow along while the selection is read aloud to you.

Earthquakes: What, Where, When, and Why

An earthquake is the shaking, rolling, or vibrating of a part of the earth's surface. This activity often lasts for only seconds. If a quake is very large, it can be felt as far away as 1,000 miles. It is a terrifying event. An earthquake can be one of the most devastating natural disasters. However, few of the thousands that occur yearly are felt by people. Even fewer cause massive destruction.

What Causes an Earthquake?

Scientists now believe that earthquakes are caused by the movement of the earth's plates. The earth's crust is divided into 20 plates. These plates move slowly past one another in opposite directions. Between any two plates is a boundary called a fault. The continual movement of the plates produces a strain on the rocks on either side of the fault. Sometimes parts of the plates become locked together and cannot move. When the strain builds to the breaking point along the fault line, the plates jerk free, causing an earthquake. Frequently, a major earthquake is followed by several smaller, less intense earthquakes called aftershocks.

Some countries that have experienced major quake activity are China, Chile, Japan, Iran, Peru, and the United States.

How Are Earthquakes Measured?

Seismologists are the scientists who study earthquakes. They measure the magnitude of a quake using a numerical scale called the Richter scale. The numbers range from 1 to 9. Quakes that register 6 or greater are major earthquakes.

If a major quake strikes a highly populated area, the death toll can be high. Buildings and roadways that are not constructed to withstand the force of a quake might, and frequently do, collapse. Gas lines often break during a quake. Sometimes fires break out, greatly adding to the damage.

Can Earthquakes Be Predicted?

Predicting earthquakes is not an easy task. Scientists study the size of past quakes and the areas along the faults where they have occurred. They also study rock movements along sections of faults by placing gauges as deep as 1,000 feet into the earth.

From their studies, scientists have learned that a longer period of time passes between major earthquakes than between minor ones. They also know that if a major earthquake has happened along a certain fault, future earthquakes most likely will occur in that area. Today, scientists can accurately predict an approximate area where a major earthquake will happen, but they cannot predict the exact time when one will strike. As technology improves, perhaps they will be able to predict the time as well. Then people in a quake zone could be alerted.

Writing

Pre-writing

You will use ideas from the selection to help you to complete two writing activities. For the first activity, you will write an informational essay about earthquakes, using information from the selection "Earthquakes: What, Where, When, and Why." For the second activity, you will write a letter to a scientist in which you request additional information about earthquakes.

Directions: Use the chart to organize what you have learned about earthquakes from the article.

What Causes Earthquakes	How Earthquakes Are Measured	How Scientists Predict Earthquakes

© Harcourt

Name _____

Pre-writing

Directions: Use the outline below to organize your letter. Use a heading that contains the address of the writer and the date. The inside address gives the name and address of the person to whom the letter is written. The greeting gives the title and name of the person addressed and ends with a colon. The body of the letter contains facts listed in logical order. The letter ends with a polite closing phrase and the handwritten signature which gives the name of the writer.

(heading) _____

_____

_____

_____

_____

_____ (inside address)

(greeting) Dear _____:

(body)

_____

_____

_____

_____

_____

_____

(closing) Sincerely,

(signature) _____

Informational Essay

Directions: You will write an informational essay about earthquakes, using information from the selection "Earthquakes: What, Where, When, and Why." Be sure to include what causes earthquakes, how they are measured, and how scientists predict them. Be sure to use words that make your meaning clear. Be sure to use the information that you read in the story.

Look at the box below. The checklist shows what your writing must have to receive your best score.

Checklist

I will earn my best score if:

⇨ My informational essay tells the causes of earthquakes.

⇨ My informational essay tells how earthquakes are measured.

⇨ My informational essay tells how scientists predict earthquakes.

⇨ My informational essay contains a title, a main idea, and detailed sentences that support the main idea.

⇨ I use words that make my meaning clear, and I do not use the same words over and over.

⇨ I spell words correctly.

⇨ I use correct punctuation and capitalization.

Letter

Directions: You will write a letter to a scientist in which you ask him or her questions that you would like to find out about earthquakes. Refer to your chart to remember what you wanted to find out about earthquakes. You may also refer to the letter form you used to organize your letter. Be sure to identify yourself. Be sure to include a greeting, a body, and a closing. Be sure that your questions are clear.

Look at the box below. The checklist shows what your writing must have to receive your best score.

Checklist

I will earn my best score if:

⇨ My questions are clear.

⇨ My letter asks the scientist for information about earthquakes.

⇨ My letter has a polite, formal tone.

⇨ My letter has a heading, an inside address, a greeting, a body, a closing, and a signature.

⇨ My proper nouns begin with a capital letter.

⇨ I spell words correctly.

⇨ I use correct punctuation and capitalization.

Name_____

Directions: Read the selection and answer the questions.

Nathan knew when he awoke to the sound of raindrops that it wasn't going to be a good day. He had to ride his bike to school because his mom had to be at work early. He heard her car pulling out.

Nathan reluctantly crawled out of bed and shook his head, trying to wake up. A nice warm shower would help him feel better, he decided. But that wasn't to be. His brother had used all the hot water, and ice water fell from the showerhead! He hurried out to dry off and warm up, but he couldn't find a clean towel. Yes, this was going to be a great day!

Nathan ate quickly, thinking about Cathie, the new girl in his class. Yesterday she had smiled at him. Today he thought he had enough courage to talk to her.

He dressed in his favorite jeans and a new T-shirt, hoping this would help turn the tide of bad luck. It didn't work. His brother, of course, had taken his raincoat. He packed himself into a "kitchen-size trash bag," as they seemed to be out of the large "outdoor" kind. He put on his bicycle helmet and pulled galoshes over his sneakers.

The ride to school wasn't fun. The torrential rain had lightened only to a steady downpour. Nathan was just one block away from school when a car swooped past and his overshoes filled with water. Not only were his feet now soaked, but his legs were so heavy that he lost his balance and fell off the bike.

Nathan had had about enough. If he hadn't been so close to school and hadn't wanted to talk to Cathie so badly, he would have turned around and gone back home.

He managed to dry off some and look a little less bedraggled as he walked into his first-period class. He saw Cathie talking to his friend David. He was about to join them when Mr. Zallin announced that all students should take their seats.

"The test will begin in a moment."

"A test! What test?" Nathan thought. "Oh no, there *was* a test scheduled for today. How could I have forgotten?"

Nathan did the best he could on the test. Then he began to think about how rotten the day had been so far. After class he didn't even try to talk to Cathie. He was afraid anything he did today would be jinxed. So far the day had been full of bad luck, and it wasn't even half over yet.

"Nathan, wait a minute," someone called. Turning, he saw it was Cathie.

"You look like you could use a friend," she said. "What's wrong?"

"Oh, nothing. It's just the rain, I guess," he said, not knowing what else to say.

"Well, I've got something that might help," she said with a smile. "Have you seen this article from today's newspaper? I've got to run to my next class, but read it. I think it will help."

"Sure. Okay. I will," Nathan said.

As Cathie hurried off, he began reading. During study period, he finished. Then he went to the library and found some joke books. Some of the jokes were so silly that he had to laugh. Others were really funny. He found himself chuckling as he walked to his last class. He felt better than he had all day. Maybe the article was right. He glanced at it again. "Laughing Matters!" was the title. Well, the sun wasn't out yet, but Nathan couldn't help thinking, "It certainly does matter."

© Harcourt

Name _____

Constructing Meaning

Use the story map to record the events of the story in order.

EVENTS

1.

2.

3.

4.

5.

6.

7.

8.

Extending Meaning

1. Does the author of the selection think laughter is important? Explain your answer.

_____

_____

_____

_____

_____

2. Choose one word from the following that you think best describes Cathie: *selfish, helpful, unconcerned.* Support your choice with information from the selection.

_____

_____

_____

_____

_____

3. Retell this story in detail.

_____

_____

_____

_____

_____

Practice Test

Directions: Choose the best answer and fill in the circle of your choice.

1. From this selection, you can tell that Cathie _____.

   (A) is sensitive to other people's feelings
   (B) does not like Nathan
   (C) wants to make Nathan jealous by talking to David
   (D) thinks only of herself

2. What is the meaning of the word *galoshes* as it is used in the fourth paragraph of the selection?

   (A) trash bags
   (B) new shoes
   (C) overshoes worn in the rain
   (D) special shoes worn while riding bicycles

3. Which of the following best states the main idea of the selection?

   (A) Nathan's bad day gets better when he takes the advice given in an article.
   (B) Nathan has a bad day that just gets worse.
   (C) A rainy day brings bad luck to Nathan.
   (D) Nathan feels his family and friends are all against him on rainy days.

4. According to the selection, which event happened first?

   (A) Nathan read a newspaper article.
   (B) Nathan put on a trash bag and galoshes.
   (C) Mr. Zallin told everyone to sit down.
   (D) Nathan talked to Cathie.

5. From this selection, you can infer that the article Nathan read was _____.

   (A) a sad story
   (B) about laughter's ability to make people sick
   (C) about laughter's ability to make people feel better
   (D) not what Nathan needed to read

6. The next time Nathan sees Cathie, he will probably _____.

   (A) ignore her completely
   (B) ask her why she was talking to David
   (C) ask her why she had to hurry off
   (D) thank her for the helpful article

© Harcourt

GO ON

7. Nathan's attitude improved from the way he felt at the beginning of the selection to the way he felt at the end. Why do you think his attitude improved?

_____

_____

_____

_____

_____

_____

_____

_____

_____

8. Summarize the general idea of this selection.

_____

_____

_____

_____

_____

_____

_____

_____

_____

STOP

Name _____

Directions: Read the selection and answer the questions.

The members of Miss Summer's class were writing poems. Each poem was a figure of speech that described something. As they finished writing, the students took turns reading their work aloud. The student who first identified the object being described in another student's poem was allowed to read his or her own poem. Perry began with this poem.

I open it like a present to give
to my little brother, who sits near
to my gift of animals that live
as I read the stories he wants to hear.

Anna guessed Perry's poem, so she read hers.

It roars at me to get out of the way
when I loaf in the house on Saturday.

It eats up the dirt and all of the dust
and growls, "Get busy! You must!
    You must!"
It pulls my mother around on its cord
and makes such a racket you can't hear
    a word.

Hal finally got that one and then read his own poem.

When I watch the parade, I wait to see
the huge golden mirrors reflecting me
from the back of the band, flashing high
as the sun burns brightly in each big eye.
"Crash!" and "Crash! We see you
    blinking!"
"Keep clapping and playing!" is what
    I'm thinking.

Reading

Constructing Meaning

1. How do you know what object Anna is describing in her poem? What clues does she give the reader?

_____

_____

_____

_____

_____

_____

_____

_____

2. What clues are most helpful to you in determining the object that Hal is describing? Explain your choices.

_____

_____

_____

_____

_____

_____

_____

Reading

Extending Meaning

1. Did you enjoy reading these poems? Why or why not?

_____

_____

_____

_____

_____

_____

2. Do you think the poets' images and descriptions provide enough clues to help the reader figure out what they are describing?

_____

_____

_____

_____

_____

_____

_____

3. Which object did you find the hardest to figure out? Explain why.

_____

_____

_____

_____

_____

_____

Reading

Practice Test

Directions: Choose the best answer and fill in the circle of your choice.

1. Anna guesses that Perry is describing _____.

   Ⓐ a toy he gives his brother
   Ⓑ the ribbon on a package
   Ⓒ a cage at the zoo
   Ⓓ a book he reads to his brother

2. The object Perry describes is compared to a _____.

   Ⓐ little boy
   Ⓑ pet dog
   Ⓒ gift to be opened
   Ⓓ door that is closed

3. Hal guesses that Anna's poem is about _____.

   Ⓐ her pet dog
   Ⓑ a vacuum cleaner
   Ⓒ kite
   Ⓓ her baby brother

4. Anna's object _____.

   Ⓐ purrs
   Ⓑ barks
   Ⓒ roars
   Ⓓ growls

5. Hal's poem describes _____.

   Ⓐ cymbals
   Ⓑ airplanes
   Ⓒ windows
   Ⓓ glasses

6. The objects in Hal's poem are compared to _____.

   Ⓐ mirrors and eyes
   Ⓑ flags carried in a parade
   Ⓒ helicopters
   Ⓓ cameras

© Harcourt

GO ON ⟩

7. What does Perry compare his object to?

_____

8. What sights and sounds does Hal use to describe his object? Use words from the poem to complete the chart.

Sights	Sounds

9. Which poet's descriptions do you think are the best? Explain your answer.

_____

_____

_____

_____

_____

_____

STOP

Directions: Follow along while this selection is read aloud to you.

Equipment for Undersea Exploration

Diving in its simplest form has probably been done since humans entered the water. As long ago as 300 B.C., the people of the eastern Mediterranean paid divers to salvage property from sunken vessels. Since then divers have used all kinds of equipment to explore the seas.

Skin Diving

Early divers had no equipment except a stone to help them sink. They were very limited in what they could accomplish underwater because they couldn't stay underwater for more than one or two minutes. This "skin diving" is still done in some parts of the world. These divers primarily gather oysters and sponges from shallow seabeds.

Diving Suits

In 1819, a German engineer, Augustus Siebe, invented a suit that was the forerunner of the diving suit used today. Siebe's suit had a layer of rubber sandwiched between two layers of fabric. It enclosed the body from the feet to the neck.

A round copper helmet was screwed onto the neck of the suit. A flexible air pipe connected the helmet to a pump on the surface of the water. Air from the pump entered the helmet through a valve that prevented it from flowing backward. A separate outlet valve on the helmet helped the diver control the amount of air in the suit as well as the ability to sink and to float to the surface of the water. By closing the valve, the diver caused the suit to inflate and to become more buoyant.

Divers' Sickness

Air pressure within Siebe's suit needed to be maintained carefully to correspond to the water pressure outside the suit. Rising to the surface too quickly could result in the "bends," a painful condition that divers even today try to avoid.

Modern Diving Suits

Self-contained diving suits were developed after Siebe's suit. They are preferred by many because the diver carries his or her own air supply and is able to swim freely. There are two kinds of self-contained suits, the rebreathing suit and the open-circuit suit.

In a rebreathing suit, the diver breathes from a rubber bag on the chest that is supplied by a cylinder of oxygen under pressure. The used oxygen passes through a chemical purifier and back to the bag to be used again. This suit has the advantage of having no stream of exhaust bubbles to reach the surface. It was used by World War II "frogmen" who attached explosives to enemy ships.

SCUBA, which stands for Self-Contained Underwater Breathing Apparatus, uses the open-circuit air apparatus. Air is carried in tanks on the diver's back. The air is supplied to the mouthpiece through a valve that opens automatically when the diver breathes. This equipment was made famous by undersea explorer Jacques Cousteau and is widely used.

© Harcourt

Pre-writing

You will use ideas from the reading passage to help you complete two writing activities. For the first activity, you will write a short article for your school newspaper that explains why one piece of underwater diving equipment is important. For the second activity, you will write a review that explains what you learned from reading the passage "Equipment for Undersea Exploration."

Directions: Use the organizer to help you organize your thoughts about underwater diving equipment. Fill in the boxes with ideas, words, or information from the passage "Equipment for Undersea Exploration."

One important piece of diving equipment is _____.

What this piece of equipment does:

Why a diver needs this piece of equipment:

What would happen if a diver did not have this piece of equipment:

Writing

Pre-writing

Directions: Use the chart below to organize your ideas about what you knew before you read "Equipment for Undersea Exploration," what you learned from the essay, and what you would still like to know about underwater diving.

What I Knew About Underwater Diving Before Reading	What I Learned from "Equipment for Undersea Exploration"	What I Would Still Like to Learn About Underwater Diving

© Harcourt

Newspaper Article

Directions: For this exercise, you will write an article explaining why you think one piece of underwater diving equipment is important. You may use the ideas you included in the graphic organizers on the previous pages. Be sure to state clearly why you think the piece of diving equipment is important. Be sure to include reasons and details that support your idea. Try to use words that make your meaning clear. Also, be sure that your article presents information in a clear and organized way.

Look at the box below. The checklist shows what your writing must have to receive your best score.

Checklist

I will earn my best score if:

⇨ My article states that a piece of underwater diving equipment is an important development.

⇨ My article gives reasons that support my main idea.

⇨ My article includes details about underwater diving equipment that support my reasons.

⇨ I use words that make my meaning clear, and I do not use the same words over and over again.

⇨ I spell words correctly.

⇨ I use correct punctuation and capitalization.

© Harcourt

Writing

Review

Directions: For this exercise, you will write a review of the essay "Equipment for Undersea Exploration." Use any ideas you included in your K-W-L chart. Be sure to state clearly what you learned from the essay. Also, explain what information you wish the essay had included. Be sure to include at least one quotation from the essay in your review. Try to use words that make your meaning clear.

Look at the box below. The checklist shows what your writing must have to receive your best score.

Checklist

I will earn my best score if:

⇨ My review states clearly what I learned from the essay "Equipment for Underwater Exploration."

⇨ My review explains what information I would have liked to find in the essay "Equipment for Underwater Exploration."

⇨ My review contains at least one quotation from the essay "Equipment for Underwater Exploration."

⇨ My review contains a main idea and detailed sentences that support the main idea.

⇨ In my review, I am careful not to repeat the same words over and over, and I use a variety of words and sentence patterns.

⇨ I spell words correctly.

⇨ I use correct punctuation and capitalization.

© Harcourt

Spelling

Find the misspelled word. If no words are spelled incorrectly, mark the answer "No mistakes."

1. (A) organize
   (B) personal
   (C) confusion
   (D) No mistakes

2. (A) accidentally
   (B) quiz
   (C) actave
   (D) No mistakes

3. (A) quantity
   (B) cruise
   (C) reduce
   (D) No mistakes

4. (A) bulletin
   (B) require
   (C) elementery
   (D) No mistakes

5. (A) sauser
   (B) allowance
   (C) secondary
   (D) No mistakes

6. (A) campaign
   (B) substence
   (C) ascent
   (D) No mistakes

7. (A) suitable
   (B) feature
   (C) auther
   (D) No mistakes

8. (A) throughout
   (B) contents
   (C) utensil
   (D) No mistakes

9. (A) beckon
   (B) varriety
   (C) walnut
   (D) No mistakes

Language

Punctuation

As you read each sentence, look for errors in punctuation. When you find a mistake, mark the letter of the line that contains the mistake. If there are no mistakes, mark the answer "No mistakes."

1. (A) I wrote a report on the
   (B) history of bread and I
   (C) earned an excellent grade.
   (D) No mistakes

2. (A) My mother appreciates
   (B) having my help
   (C) in the kitchen
   (D) No mistakes

3. (A) "Have you ever baked
   (B) a loaf of bread
   (C) by yourself?" Micah asked.
   (D) No mistakes

4. (A) I found hundreds of recipes
   (B) for bread in an old
   (C) cookbook, I tried ten of them.
   (D) No mistakes

5. (A) I said to my friend
   (B) "I have several suggestions
   (C) for bread recipes."
   (D) No mistakes

6. (A) I can spread cream cheese on
   (B) this bagel, or I can spread
   (C) butter on it.
   (D) No mistakes

7. (A) I have become an excellent
   (B) cook because I always read
   (C) recipes carefully
   (D) No mistakes

8. (A) In a cookbook
   (B) I found a recipe for
   (C) cinnamon rolls.
   (D) No mistakes

9. (A) I sent one of my favorite
   (B) recipes to my grandmother and she
   (C) sent one of hers to me.
   (D) No mistakes

Capitalization

As you read each sentence, look for errors in capitalization. When you find a mistake, mark the letter of the line that contains the mistake. If there are no mistakes, mark the answer "No mistakes."

1. (A) My uncle, who lives in
    (B) New Orleans, Louisiana, is
    (C) a well-known archaeologist.
    (D) No mistakes

2. (A) While Uncle Frank was working
    (B) at a site in Africa,
    (C) he met aunt Jane.
    (D) No mistakes

3. (A) I enjoy visiting the
    (B) New York museum of Archaeology
    (C) whenever I can.
    (D) No mistakes

4. (A) I studied archaeology
    (B) while I was in sixth grade
    (C) at Parker Elementary school.
    (D) No mistakes

5. (A) "Well," Mr. Berg said, "This
    (B) is the first time I have
    (C) been to Europe for an
        archaeological dig."
    (D) No mistakes

6. (A) I once read a book about ancient
    (B) Mayan ruins written by l. r. Boyd
    (C) and illustrated by J. D. Beck.
    (D) No mistakes

7. (A) One of the most famous
    (B) underwater sites is the site
    (C) where the *titanic* sank.
    (D) No mistakes

8. (A) Ms. Lee said, "Students, take
    (B) out your English books
    (C) and your journals."
    (D) No mistakes

9. (A) My favorite book about
        archaeology
    (B) is called *Discovering By Uncovering*.
    (C) It explains every aspect of digging.
    (D) No mistakes

10. (A) When I walk past the construction
    (B) on Mercer street, I wonder if any
    (C) artifacts lie beneath the broken
        ground.
    (D) No mistakes

Name _____

Usage

This is a test on usage. Choose the best way to write the underlined part of the sentence. If it is correct the way it is written, mark "No mistakes."

1. Last *Cinco de Mayo*, my grandparents have a party.

   (A) has
   (B) will have
   (C) had
   (D) No mistakes

2. Me and my family attended the fiesta.

   (A) My family and me
   (B) My family and I
   (C) I and my family
   (D) No mistakes

3. The piñata swung from a tree limb.

   (A) through
   (B) with
   (C) after
   (D) No mistakes

4. The children sharing the prizes in the piñata.

   (A) shares
   (B) shared
   (C) will sharing
   (D) No mistakes

5. My grandfather played his guitar for my brother and I.

   (A) my brother and me
   (B) me and my brother
   (C) I and my brother
   (D) No mistakes

6. My two younger brothers clapped their hands.

   (A) more younger
   (B) most young
   (C) more young
   (D) No mistakes

7. All of the children played good together.

   (A) more good
   (B) more well
   (C) well
   (D) No mistakes

8. I counted ten lesser people than my mother did.

   (A) fewer
   (B) more less
   (C) few
   (D) No mistakes

9. Before we left, I found a set of car keys.

   (A) find
   (B) will find
   (C) finds
   (D) No mistakes

10. I asked everyone who's keys they were.

    (A) whos
    (B) whos'
    (C) whose
    (D) No mistakes

© Harcourt

Theme 6 • *Language*